Memories *of* a Mountain Educator

Memories *of* a Mountain Educator

FROM A ONE-ROOM SCHOOLHOUSE
TO A COLLEGE CLASSROOM

PAUL F. TAYLOR

COMMONWEALTH BOOK COMPANY

2020

To my wife, Sue Ann Taylor, my loyal and faithful companion for forty-three years as well as to all my students, especially those I taught at Augusta College.

PAUL F. TAYLOR was born in Warm Springs, Georgia. While still a small child, his family moved to Pineville, Kentucky where he graduated from Pineville High School with honors. After attending Berea College for three years, he taught in a one-room school deep in the hills of Harlan County and later was teacher and principal in a three-room school in Bell County. Taylor finished his udergraduate degree at Eastern Kenucky University and later completed a M.A. and a Ph.D. at the University of Kentucky. He then embarked on a long and distinguished teaching career of 27 years at Augusta College in Augusta, Georgia.

Table of Contents

Introduction

You might say that I was born to teach, that teaching was in my blood. My father, Vernon Floyd Washington Taylor, was a member of a pioneer family in Harlan County, Kentucky where his grandfather, William J. Taylor, lived and practiced law in the early years of the nineteenth century. However, my father left Harlan County and in the mid-1920s found himself in the middle of Georgia. It was there, near Warm Springs, Georgia, that he met my mother, Clara Emma Miller, whose parents lived on and farmed a red clay piece of land in the valley section of Talbot County. Following their marriage in 1925, my father, who was also an itinerant preacher, pastored churches at places like Warm Springs, Blue Ridge, Subligna, and Red Bud. Soon thereafter, following the birth of my sister Rachel at Blue Ridge and my birth at Warm Springs, my parents left Georgia to settle in Pineville, county seat of Bell County, Kentucky. In Pineville, three more additions, Louise, Emma, John Wesley, graced the Taylor household. And it just so happened, or maybe it was predestined or perhaps it was just in our bloodline, that four out of five, Rachel, Louise, John Wesley and myself, turned to teaching as a profession.

It was in Pineville that I was educated in the elementary, junior and senior high schools. I was an apt enough pupil to get double-promoted in the elementary grades and when I finished Pineville High in 1944, I had a star by my name in the graduation program, meaning I had finished in the upper third of my graduating class. I probably could have been a better student for I remember one of my high school teachers telling my mother one day in the old J.J. Newberry store, located across from the Bell County Courthouse, that "Paul" could do a lot better if only he applied himself. I had no real excuse for not being a better student since I did not participate in athletics. After school I hurried home to help out with chores like slopping the hog, milking the cow, cleaning out the chicken house, and hoeing corn. During my high school years, I literally walked all over Pineville delivering the *Knoxville News-Sentinel* newspaper.

With my high school graduation behind me, I left Pineville for Berea College without the faintest inkling of what I wanted to do with my life. My recollection is that my two chief interests in those years, in order, were (1) sports, i.e., basketball; (2) girls. Getting an education was somewhere on the back burner. The admonition of my high school teacher "if only he applied himself" came hauntingly back to me at the end of my sophomore year. I had not yet found myself academically.

And so I left Berea College to begin a teaching career that would last off-and-on but mostly on until my retirement as a college professor in 1994. Admittedly, I was not all that unhappy to leave Berea in those days for the college was well known for its enforcement of a strict code of conduct on its students. For example, eating establishments like "Little Mama's" on Short Street were off limits to students as well as places like the theater in west end of Berea. Cars were not allowed for most students, students could not visit Richmond and Lexington and, of all things, girls had to be in dormitories at a specified time. Of course, as students, we ventured out to west end to the picture show where we sat in the balcony. The management was gracious enough to blink the house lights when a Berea College official entered so that we could slump down in our seats to escape recognition. More often than not we ordered "Little Mama's" pizzas from the walk-up window adjacent to the front door of that popular hangout. If we were late getting a co-ed back to her dorm, she was "campused," or placed on restriction, meaning she was not allowed "late privileges."

I
Sampson

My search for a job took me to the offices of the Harlan County Board of Education, then located in the historic Harlan County courthouse in downtown Harlan. (The courthouse was famous for the many United Mine Workers' rallies held there as well as for trials involving union members. In its hallways gun battles took place over a decade earlier) In a sense I was returning to my roots for my father, my grandfather, James Buchanan Taylor, and my great-grandfather, as mentioned previously, were all Harlan Countians. Superintendent of the Harlan County system at that time was James A. Cawood for whom Cawood High School is named. Director of Personnel was Cecil Thornton. Following a brief meeting with Superintendent Cawood, I was ushered into the offices of Mr. Thornton who explained that there was only one position open, a one-room school at Sampson, located at the head of Martin's Fork, one of the tributaries of the Cumberland River. I needed a job even if it was in one of the most remote sections of the county so after a moment's deliberation, I told Mr. Thornton I'd take it. After filling out the necessary forms, I was shown outside where I climbed into the cab of a Board of Education truck for the journey to Sampson. In back of the truck were all the necessary school supplies—books, chalk, desks, a teacher's desk and chair, and a water bucket and dipper.

On a perfect late summer day in southeastern Kentucky, the truck driver and I headed out US 421. After we had gone several miles, we turned off the hard road to follow a very narrow, almost one-lane dirt road. On both sides of the road were various kinds of rail fences which needed repair and different kinds of wire fences. As we traveled along it came to me that we were in what has commonly been called the "boondocks" or "boonies." Houses were few, most were located near the country lane, all were located far apart. Surrounding the houses were densely wooded hills. Alongside the dirt road was a picturesque creek. Near most houses was a cleared area where vegetable gardens had grown. Near a few of the houses was an enclosed pasture where cows and horses grazed. Most of the houses were of simple frame construction, unpainted, with porches and chimneys. A few were Kentucky log houses. To one side or in back of the houses stood the unpainted primitive outhouse. As I sat in the cab of the Board of Education truck, lost in thought, I pondered the experience which was about to unfold before me. It also occurred to me that I was perhaps viewing the houses from which my students would come the next day.

Finally, after a bouncing truck ride which lasted about an hour, but the time seemed a lot longer than that, the one-room frame unpainted schoolhouse loomed just ahead on the left-hand side of the road. As the truck screeched to a stop in front of the school, I climbed down out of the cab to take a better look at what would be my domain in the hills for the next nine months. Nestled beneath a grove of Kentucky hardwoods, interspersed by a few evergreens, the building, open underneath, was under-pinned by posts with steps leading up from the ground into the schoolroom. Centered in front was a door with two windows on each side of the building affording the only light. I immediately sensed that on dark, overcast days, common in the hills, especially since the school was surrounded by the woods, light inside would be a problem. Behind the schoolhouse stood two outhouses, one for the boys, the other for the girls. In the center of the modest wooden building stood a chimney.

While the truck driver dumped the school supplies out on the ground, I climbed the steps, unlocked the door, walked into the room where my virginal teaching experiences began. The centerpiece of the room was a pot-bellied stove which during winter months would furnish heat. In front of the room, stretching nearly from one wall to the opposite wall, was the blackboard. At the rear of the room were shelves for the water bucket and dipper and the children's lunches. Completing the trip around my sanctuary, I walked outside where the truck driver was about to finish unloading the truck. Apparently his job was to load, drive, unload. It fell to me to transfer everything into the schoolhouse.

As the truck lurched off down the road up which we had driven a few moments earlier, I busied myself with getting the schoolroom ready for school. Picking up the desks, books, and school supplies, I began to carry them inside. Placing my desk at the front of the room, I arranged the students' desks in several rows from front to back. Books to be handed out to the pupils the next day were stacked neatly on my desk. At that instant it dawned on me! I had contracted not only to be a teacher but a custodian, a nurse, a builder of fires when the weather turned cold, a playground supervisor and an athlete at recess all rolled into one.

While getting things ready for the first day of school, I suddenly sensed that I was not alone. Pausing to glance up from my work, I looked into the eyes of a young sandy-headed mountain man with ruddy complexion dressed in overalls. I stopped, we exchanged "howdies," and then came the obvious question: "Are you the new teacher?" I responded that I was and that school would begin tomorrow. My new acquaintance whose name was Fielding Hensley then informed that "they" had "run off" several of my predecessors in the profession. Raising my frame to its full six feet two inches, I looked Fielding squarely in the eye. "Well, I have been sent up here to teach the full school term and I plan to do just that." Fielding and I exchanged a few more words before he trudged off down the road. With his departure, I finished getting the schoolroom ready and locked the door.

As the sun dipped low in the western sky, I set off down the road looking for a place to spend the night. Since Sampson was out in the "sticks," it was necessary for me to board in the community. I did not own a car and if I had it would not have done me much good for the dirt road became a sea of mud during rainy and snowy weather. With my suitcase in hand, I stopped at the first house I came to, a modest frame building with a porch and knocked on the door. A pretty young woman whom I reckoned to be in her twenties came to the door. Clutching her skirts on either side were two little girls, blonde and blue-eyed, both of whom I greeted as two of my pupils the next day. Introducing myself, I inquired if she had a spare room. She responded that she would be glad for me to stay the night but that her coal miner-husband worked nights. Hearing that I knew it would not be proper for me to spend a single night in the Marcum household. Thanking Mrs. Marcum, I continued my quest.

By that time the shadows were lengthening as darkness began to creep into the hollows of Martin's Fork. As I approached the next house, I noticed the dim outlines of several people on the porch. Leaving the road, I made my way to a house of Howards, one of the most common names in Harlan County. By that time all but one of the porch occupants had disappeared inside the house. But I felt several pairs of eyes focused on me from within as I stopped in the yard. Once again I introduced myself as I repeated that I was looking for a place to spend the night. Mr. Howard told me that while he did not have an extra bed I could stay the night if I did not mind sleeping with one of the boys. Having run out of options for the day, I thanked him. He showed me inside and on my first night in Sampson, I ate alone by lamplight at a table in the kitchen. While I do not recall what I ate that evening, soon after I had finished my meal, I was shown my room where I retired. Later I discovered that as soon as darkness filled the region, most people went to bed. Thus it became my custom the next few months to go to bed around eight o'clock or by dark, whichever came first. In a strange land, in a strange house, in a strange bed, although fatigued, I did not drop off to sleep at once. And before I did, one of the boys, C.E., came and climbed into bed and got over against the wall.

The first day of school in the fall was exciting. Greeting me upon my arrival at the one-room schoolhouse were around thirty-five boys and girls, grades one through eight. Some of the little ones were accompanied by their parents. There they were—scrubbed and clean, shining faces, combed hair, new school clothes which were bought a weekend or two earlier on a trip to Harlan town, county seat of Harlan County. One of my oldest boys, nearly as tall as I, was lanky, dark-haired Johnny Howard, C.E.'s brother, my bunk mate of the previous evening. Big for his age and older too, Johnny was a seventh grader. My oldest student and probably the prettiest was Mary Hensley, Fielding's sister, an eighth grader. Mary had light-brown shoulder length hair, a round face, china doll complexion, and sparkling brown eyes. Clifford Wilson was a fourth grader with an effervescent smile. A handsome chap, Clifford had dark brown eyes and hair. Then there was blond, mischievous Junior Long whom I later found out would not be in school when there was something better to do like hunting. A twentieth century version of Daniel Boone, Junior would rather let the girls do the spelling while he did the shooting. Those were the students who stood out. The others were mountain children who came to school rather regularly until Christmas. After the holidays and the onset of winter weather which brought cold and snow to the hills, attendance dropped off dramatically. With the coming of spring, some of those whom I had not seen since December trickled back to school, while others did not attempt to travel the muddy road. And in keeping with my admonition to Fielding, when May rolled around, Sampson school was still in session.

The first day of school passed rather uneventfully. At recess, blonde, blue-eyed, freckle-faced Mary Wilson, who was twelve, came up to ask if I had found a place to stay. When I answered that I had not, she told me that her mother had said I could stay with them if I did not mind sharing a bed with sixteen-year-old Oscar when he was at home. Mary also told me that her mother was afraid for her to walk off the mountain by herself to school. At the end of the first day of school, I climbed the mountain with Mary to what was to be my boarding place for the school term.

My new "home" away from home was a three-room log house next to another log house. (I used to say log cabin but stopped after Knott County's Verna Mae Slone brought me up short one day. As I visited in her log house, I said something about a log cabin. Instantly she interrupted to correct me. Something I shall always remember). The two front rooms were both bedrooms. In one were two double beds, one shared by Mary and her mother, the other was father Daniel's bed. In the adjoining room was a double bed which I shared with Oscar when he was not out "tomcatting" around. The room with two double beds had a fireplace around which we sat on cold nights after supper listening to the "Suppertime Frolic" from WJJD in Chicago on a battery-powered radio. The thing about a fireplace being the only source of heat was that a person burned up on the front side while the back side froze. At the back of the house was the kitchen which contained a stove and table and chairs around which we sat for morning and evening meals. Since my abode was high up on the mountain, wood was used for heating and cooking purposes instead of coal in Harlan County, which was famous as the "home of good coal."

Next to my boarding place was a log house occupied by an elderly white-haired mountain man called Uncle John who lived alone but ate all his meals at Daniel's table. Uncle John Wilson was a distinguished-looking old fellow who, despite lack of formal education, was pretty well-versed about what was going on in the world. Somewhat hard of hearing, Uncle John and I on many afternoons when I arrived "home" from school would sit on his porch where we discussed the news and current events. When it was time for the late afternoon news, Uncle John and I would go inside where he tuned up his battery-powered radio. Afterwards we returned to the porch to discuss the news until suppertime. Chief topics of conversation during those afternoon sessions on the front porch included the Truman Administration, the onset of the Cold War and the post-war unrest which permeated the United States in the post World War II years. I thoroughly enjoyed my conversations with Uncle John for he was certainly more in tune with what was going on outside the hollows of Harlan than most residents of the area.

My "home" away from home was clean and comfortable. Some nights, I had the bed to myself because Oscar did not come home. Other nights he came in well into the night and crawled into bed with me. I always heard him come in since the rest of his family was usually in bed. One night Daniel came in rather late. Obviously he was drunk because he was ranting, raving, cursing despite the efforts of his spouse to calm him down. Finally she got him in bed where he lapsed into a stupor.

I ate breakfast and supper at "home." Like Mary I carried a lunch to school. The diet was always the same with no attention paid to fatty foods or cholesterol. For breakfast there were biscuits, large and heavy, fat-back bacon, sometimes referred to as a streak-of-lean, gravy, fried potatoes. For lunch I had a biscuit sandwich of fat-back. Then for supper there was skillet cornbread or hardtack, thick and coarse, gravy, beans and potatoes.

The menu rarely varied from one day to the next. Sanitary facilities were provided by an unsanitary outhouse a ways from the house. At night, rather than a trek to the outhouse, I just went outside and relieved myself off the end of the porch. It seemed as if that was customary for the folks where I stayed.

I quickly settled into the school year, spending my days trying to teach all the children in grades one through eight. Afternoons were passed on Uncle John's porch or in his house on colder days, and evenings were spent in Daniel's house listening to the radio following supper in the kitchen.

My normal routine was to leave Sampson right after school on Friday afternoon and walk across the mountain into the company town of the Black Star Coal Corporation at Alva. Once I had crossed the mountain, I followed the tracks traveled by coal cars leading to the mine's drift mouth which was cut into the side of the mountain. After making my way around the tracks, I arrived at the mantrip which took the miners down into the camp after they had finished work for the day. On many a Friday afternoon I climbed on the mantrip to ride down the mountain with coal miners who gave me curious stares as we descended. From the mantrip I walked down the railroad tracks to the Black Star Company commissary, going inside when it was cold. I usually grabbed a snack of crackers and soda pop while I waited for my father to come from Pineville to take me home in his car. When my dad was tied up, I caught the bus which ran down Pucketts Creek and crossed the Cumberland River at Blackmont. There I waited inside a honky-tonk at the end of the bridge for the Greyhound bus from Harlan to take me into Pineville. When the weather was cold, I wore an overcoat and hat. On one occasion, while waiting for the bus, a truck stopped to pick me up. Since the cab was full, I climbed in back as the truck sped off down Highway 119. While I was trying to get settled my hat flew off down the highway. Before I could pound on the cab to tell the driver what had happened, a vehicle stopped to retrieve my hat from the middle of the highway. That truck ride cost me a fairly new felt hat.

It was good being home each weekend for two reasons. First, I got to take the first all-over bath in a week. At my "home" away from home, I usually took a sponge bath during the week. A hot tub bath on Friday night was quite exhilarating after a week of sponge baths. Also, it was good to put my feet under my mother's table to eat a square meal, a real break from the monotonous diet of the week. Fried chicken, homemade biscuits, cream chicken gravy along with assorted veggies was food for the soul after eating beans, potatoes and hardtack for a week.

On Sunday afternoon my father drove me back to Black Star where I would retrace my steps along the railroad tracks to the mantrip. If the mantrip was not running, I would climb the mountain to the mine, walk across the mountain into the valley where Sampson was located. Then I climbed yet another mountain to my boarding place. On pretty fall and spring afternoons, the hike was delightful for I loved the hills and did not mind walking them.

While my usual route in and out of Sampson was walking across to Black Star, the mountain on which I stayed was on the Virginia side of the county. One Friday in the springtime of the year, Daniel guided me across the mountain into the tiny community of Ewing, Virginia where I caught the bus into Middlesboro, then on into Pineville. The trek across into Virginia was spectacular and historical for I was traversing the region traveled by pioneers of old—Dr. Thomas Walker, John Finley, Daniel Boone and the "Long Hunters."

One winter weekend a snowstorm hit the hollows of Martin's Fork, covering the terrain with over a foot of snow. Suddenly I was snowbound with no way out since I was not prepared to hike the hills through deep snow. So I had to spend the weekend, and it was a long weekend, huddled around the fireplace in the Wilson's log house. That weekend was almost like a lost weekend for I had to go two weeks in a row without an all-over bath. A cold wave followed the storm so not many of the children made it to school. The few that did spent the day with me clustered around the fire in the pot-bellied stove. On these days ice covered the windows on the inside of the schoolhouse.

By the next weekend, the weather had moderated somewhat. So on Friday afternoon after school, I began my trip across the mountain to Black Star. It was a cold but sunny afternoon and since some of the snow had melted, I experienced little difficulty until I had nearly reached the top of the mountain. As I carefully made my way through the snow which seemed deeper now, all at once I plunged into a snow drift up to my arm pits. Was I ever surprised? Without panicking, I began floundering and thrashing around trying to get a firm footing beneath the deep snow. After what seemed to be an interminable length of time, but was actually only two or three minutes, I was able to extricate myself from the snow to continue my journey to the top and down the other side to Black Star.

It was especially good getting home that weekend both for Mom's good home cooking and the first all-over bath I'd had in two weeks. Thankfully I did not get snowed in anymore that winter.

Imagine if you will a young man with only two years of college and with no teacher training courses, trying to teach a roomful of children in grades one through eight. To say the least it was an unenviable task for which I was paid an annual salary of $1004.00.

Before I could teach the children, I first had to get accustomed to their vocabulary. Now I had lived in the mountains for most of my life so I was used to some of the hill country vernacular. For example, I had heard "ain't" and even "hain't" for is not. Other words used by the children were "ourn" for ours, "hern" for hers, and "hisn" for his. Then there was "shore" for sure, "we'uns," "nary," "ary," and "deviled" or "deviling." The latter word was somewhat new to me. I had heard "bedeviled" but they said "deviled." When I asked what that meant, I was told that if someone was "deviling" you, it meant they were teasing you. Another word used by the mountain folk was "hiney." When I paddled a boy, I spanked his "hiney." And if someone wanted to ask you how you were, they said, "How air (are) you?"

Mountain folk also used other expressions which I had not heard much. If they did not recall a particular thing or "thang," a common response would nearly always be, "I disremember." Or more often, they would say with a twang, "I don't recollect." Again when they had nothing to say about a particular matter, instead of saying, "no comment," they uttered such phrases as "I ain't got no compliments to make about hit."

As I became more acquainted with the language of the hills, I began my task to try to teach my pupils the proper way to speak and write. When the school term ended in May I don't know if I had fully achieved my mission for old habits die hard. And when they returned to their homes, more often than not, they heard their parents using the same old manner of speech.

Since phonics were not the rage, my method of teaching reading, long ago considered archaic, was through memorization. The first graders read a page over and over until they knew it by heart. Every morning I would line my first graders up at the front of the room for reading while the other pupils worked on their lessons at their desks. Sometimes Mary, my eighth grader, who was an excellent student, would help me with the little ones. Reading was always first in the morning, then spelling. My approach to teaching then, and it remained that way through the years, was to emphasize reading, writing and spelling. If a pupil could read well, write and spell well, it was my feeling that he or she would do well in school. So every day, in grades one through eight, each student received a good dose of reading, writing, and spelling. Back then I focused on the basics which returned as a current trend in education in recent years.

As time allowed, I also included arithmetic as long as it was basic stuff since that subject was always my weakest. I could usually handle math through the eighth grade. And I also included geography and history which left little time for science. (My emphasis on geography extended into my tenure as a college professor for in my United States history classes I nearly always gave map quizzes) I'll be the first to admit that I did not get around to all the subjects every day. I was in an impossible situation for a novice teacher but I did make an effort to give each grade as much instruction as I could manage. As the school year went along, my students and parents, when I came in contact with the latter, seemed satisfied with what I was doing. As for the children, I showed an interest in them from the start and as time passed, I grew to love each one and they seemed to like me. Growing up in the mountains, I was able to adapt quickly to the children and their environment.

On Friday afternoons I always closed the week with a spelling bee. The students enjoyed those and in grades where there were several students, the competition was keen to be the last to sit down. The younger pupils who were not ready for spelling gave rapt attention to their sisters, brothers and friends to see who was the best speller in school.

When I taught at Sampson, I was unaware of any law banning corporal punishment. If a student was unruly, disobedient, "sassed" the teacher, paddling was allowed. Now I had promised Fielding my first day at Sampson that I planned to be around for the end of school in May. Early in the fall, I asked Johnny Howard, one of my boys, at whose house I had spent my first night in Sampson, to make me a paddle. Johnny said he would so a few days later he brought me an outstanding homemade paddle with a long handle which fit my hand quite nicely. It had grooves up and down and crosswise from one end to the other. Johnny had gone to some pains to make his teacher a fine paddle. At first I kept the paddle on my desk, then I would carry it around the schoolroom to tap a student on the shoulder if he or she was talking instead of studying spelling words for the Friday afternoon spelling bee. The day came, however, when I had to use the paddle for the first time. Ironically, I had to paddle Johnny for misbehaving. He leaned over the desk as I applied about a dozen first-rate licks which could be heard outside and down the road. Johnny flinched, but since he was the biggest boy in school, he shed no tears. From that time on, most of the boys were well-behaved. They reasoned that if I dared paddle Johnny, I certainly would not hesitate to spank them if necessary. Of course, I never paddled a girl. When girls did something they were told not to do, the usual punishment was to keep them in at recess. Most of my girls were pretty good in school. For the remainder of the year, the paddle remained on my desk as a silent reminder of the consequences of misconduct.

The kids always looked forward to recess and lunch. Since I was the teacher-principal, I gave them both morning and afternoon recess. To show them that I was human after all, I joined in and played with them at recess. Adjoining the school which did not have a suitable playground because of rocks, boulders and trees, was a farm lot used as a pasture. Surrounded by a split-rail fence, the pasture was mostly free of rocks. At recess the bigger boys and I crossed over the fence to play with a football I supplied. By the way, we were not trespassers for the owner of the property gave us permission to use the lot. We had some rousing games at recess and it was during those contests that I came to fully understand and appreciate the old Andy Griffith rendition of "What it was, was football." For it became a real challenge to catch the ball and run, all the while dodging pursuers, without stepping in and on the cow chips which littered the pasture. The boys really got excited when their teacher got the ball.

The mountain children also taught their teacher a brand new game, one with which I was not familiar. It was called "Antney over," and was played with a hard rubber ball. Of unknown origin, the game, probably played throughout the antebellum south, was also called "Antony over," "Andy over," "Annie over," "Ante over," "Anthony over," and "Anty over." The rules of the game were simple: The older pupils chose sides as numerically equal and physically equal as possible. I usually wound up on one side and most of my bigger boys and girls were on the other side. Once the two sides were chosen one group got on one side of the schoolhouse, the other group on the opposite side. Whoever had the ball would yell, "Antney," someone on the other side would respond, "over." The ball was then thrown over the schoolhouse. Whoever caught the ball would run around one end of the building and try to hit someone with the ball. The "hit" person became a member of the opposite side and the game continued. Each side took turns throwing the ball as cries of "Antney" and then "over" filled the air. The game was very intense and physically strenuous. Of course, "teacher" was a favorite target throughout with the game being won by the side which scored the most hits. It was a rare occasion when one group "hit" all those on the other side. I enjoyed all games played with the children. In turn they got a big kick out of seeing their teacher run and play as hard as they did. When recess and lunch ended, I was all "business" back inside. The students always knew that and responded well most of the time.

From days spent at Sampson, several incidents occurred which made a lasting impression on me. One sunny morning in the springtime of the year, after school had taken up for the day, the door opened and in walked Junior Long, my "Daniel Boone" type. Glancing up, my eyes met his and we exchanged smiles. Since I had not seen Junior for a few days he seemed a bit embarrassed as he took his seat near the back of the room. He had no sooner sat down when an unpleasant odor began to drift over the room. Immediately I knew that Junior and a certain striped, loathesome animal had made contact. The room was warm which seemed to intensify the odor. Other pupils glanced around as I walked back to Junior's desk. I spoke and told him I was glad to see him. I then asked what he had been doing. Junior answered, "huntin." I already knew what he was hunting but I asked the question anyway. "Junior, what have you been hunting?"

"Skunks."

Did you catch any?"

"Yep."

"Well, Junior, why didn't you clean up and change clothes before coming to school?"

"I dunno."

By that time I knew that it would not be a normal school day if Junior stayed. I hated to do it but I told him to go home, wash up, change clothes, and come back. Junior said he would and sure enough, the next day found him back in school, all cleaned with clean clothes on. Junior was a bright and likeable kid, he just loved the out-of-doors. And like many mountain children whose parents had little or no education, Junior was not motivated at home to go to school.

Another episode which I shall always remember involved the ever-smiling Clifford Wilson. Now Clifford was a boy after my own heart. He was always there, on time, even when the weather was bad. He always had a clean, scrubbed, shiny face, neatly combed hair and clean, ironed clothes. Always polite and mannerly, Clifford was the kind who could win your heart to become teacher's "pet." One day at recess Clifford fell and skinned his knee on a rock on the playground. Tears streaming down his face, he came to me for aid and comfort. Taking my first aid kit, I started to pull up Clifford's pant leg so I could cleanse and apply medication to the wound. At once he began tugging at the bottom of his britches, all the while begging me to stop. I insisted that before I could treat his wound I would have to yank up his pants. In an agitated tone, he pled for me to stop. Finally after minutes of earnest persuasion, he relented. When I raised his britches leg I discovered why he did not want me to tend his wound. His leg was dingy and dirty; it looked like it had not seen soap and water for weeks, maybe months. I tried not to let on but I was surprised for he always looked so clean and his freckled countenance always shone. Understandably he did not want his teacher to see his grimy leg. Unlike my mother, who was a welfare worker in Bell County, Kentucky for many years, I did not tell Clifford that he should wash all over because soap was cheap and water was plentiful. After the bruised knee incident, I always wondered if Clifford had gone home and washed his leg.

Another incident of my days at Sampson school which fascinated me was a tale of the children that a "peeping tom" was forever lurking in and around the schoolhouse. Named John Henry, the word was that this adult male roamed at large in the woods, popping up here and there to watch people, houses, the schoolhouse from a distance. Completely harmless and apparently mentally retarded, John Henry, according to the children, shadowed themselves and I around the schoolhouse from time to time. I must confess that I never saw the man but on more than one occasion during the school year, the children, at recess and lunch, would point to a spot in the woods and yell, "there he is, there's John Henry." When that happened, I peered in the direction they were pointing but I did not see him in the dense forest surrounding the school. The children seemed to know where to look and they always said they saw him. When they screamed out, John Henry took off to another spot in the hills. I later learned that he was related to the Sampson post-mistress who was kin to the woman of the house where I stayed. Come to think of it, Mary's mother did not seem to be all that bright. Since my pupils always made a big thing out of seeing John Henry, I wish that I had gotten a glimpse of him before I left Sampson school. Certainly he was a community oddity who, from the reaction of the children, was the laughing-stock of the area.

As the beautiful autumn days gave way to the cold, dark, dreary days of winter, school was not the place to be. While winter days are shorter, in the hills they seemed even shorter. When the sun did shine, the mountains kept sunshine from penetrating the valley except for a few brief moments. Darkness in the hills came early in the winter. On cold, cloudy, foggy days, the mountains were especially foreboding. Yet I was at school early in the morning so that I could kindle a fire in the big, pot-bellied stove. On the coldest days, when ice and snow blanketed the hollows, the roaring fire made the stove red-hot on the outside. Very few children made it to school on those days. The ones who braved the elements and I clustered around the stove trying to keep warm. Once you got away from the stove, the room was frigid. On the coldest days, even though the fire blazed away, the ice-covered windows on the inside of the school remained frozen as did water in the bucket on the shelf. It was hard for me to teach on those days as well as for the children to learn. So we just tried to stay warm.

The cold, snowy, rainy days of winter turned the road in and out of Sampson into a quagmire. If I had owned a car it would have been impossible for me to navigate the deep ruts of mud which covered the road. In fact, from just about Christmas until the coming of spring, travel by car in and out of the community came to a standstill. The folks who lived in the area drove their cars as far as conditions permitted, parked and traveled the rest of the way on foot. The mud was so deep that it was almost asking too much of the children, especially the little ones, to walk to school. A few of the bigger pupils always came. By the time they reached the little schoolhouse, their shoes were caked and their clothes at the bottom were streaked with black mountain mud.

Following several months of cold wintry weather, spring was always welcomed. As the mountains burst forth into the pinks and reds of the red buds, the pink and white of the dogwoods, the purple of the rhododendron, the delicate pink of the mountain laurel, it was almost as if winter never happened. Almost overnight the cold, sunless days of winter were replaced by the warm sun-splashed days of spring.

While attendance picked back up, it never reached what it was during the first days of school back in September. It was hard for me to remain enthusiastic when both the children and their parents seemed disinterested in school and education. Mary Hensley, my lone eighth-grade student, was a bright girl who should have gone across the mountain to high school. I talked to her several times about getting out of the hollow to further her education. Neither she nor her parents seemed interested. Most of the boys and girls, upon completion of the eighth grade, if they completed that, were content to remain at Sampson. The girls married at an early age, the boys went to work in the mines with their fathers. Coal miners' daughters married coal miners' sons, they settled down in the hollow to conceive and birth more coal miners. They seemed "sot" in their ways. That was the pattern of their lives for years and years and I soon saw I was not about to change it.

As the spring days grew longer, I found I could spend more time at home on Sundays before heading back to Sampson and still reach where I was boarding before dark. One Sunday afternoon darkness almost overtook me before I had climbed the mountain where I was staying. As I walked the path beside the gurgling mountain stream which I had traveled many times since September, I looked ahead to see the dim outline of a man coming toward me. When I got closer, I saw that he was carrying a gun, a common sight in the Kentucky mountains. When we were nearly abreast, I recognized Fred Napier, the father of two of my boys whom I had paddled. As he stopped before me, nearly blocking my path, I realized that my heart was thumping rapidly in my chest. The following conversation ensued:

"Howdy, teacher. Gettin' in kinda late this evening, ain't ye?"

"Yes, I guess I am at that."

"You learning them there children anything?"

"Yes, sir, I hope so. At least I'm trying."

As our chat continued Fred leaned the stock of his gun on the ground while he rested against the barrel. Meanwhile, I smelled the pungent odor of Kentucky "mountain spirits" on the breath of my "friend," while I wondered what words were going to pass between his lips next.

"Wal, teacher, I jus' want ye to know that you have learnt them there boys of mine more than any other teacher we've had up hyar."

"Thank you, Fred. I've been trying to teach them, I know that."

"Well, ye have and what's more, my boys told me ye gave 'em a whupping. I know they 'served it alright. And, teacher, lemme tell you this, anytime they need a whupping, you whup 'em. And when they git home, I'll give 'em another whupping."

When Fred spoke those words, I thanked him and began to breathe a bit easier even though he picked up his gun and held it in his hand. At that moment I began to realize that maybe he was on my side and wasn't going to shoot me after all. As he stepped to one side, Fred said, "Well, teacher, I reckon you best git on up the mountain, 'cause it 'jes about dark." So I told him good evening and headed up the hill. After making a few more steps, I looked around to determine Fred's whereabouts. There was no need for me to panic for he was trudging on down the trail whistling and carrying his gun over his shoulder.

Seeing men carrying guns in the hills of Harlan was not unusual. Several decades earlier Harlan County had gained the nickname "Bloody Harlan" because of the frequency with which its residents not only carried guns but used them. The county had a high incidence of murders; blood feuds were common place. Then in the coal mine wars of the 1930s as coal miners attempted to join the United Mine Workers of America, ambushes often erupted as the "gun thugs" of the coal operators tried to dissuade miners from joining the union. The coal miners often responded with their own weapons. Shootouts were the norm. Differences among mountain people were often settled at the point of a gun. Violence abounded in the hills. So when I encountered Fred near dark on that lonely mountain path I did not know quite what to expect especially since I had whipped his boys. While I did not use the paddle often, when I did use it, it was absolutely necessary. Throughout the school term, none of the parents of boys I spanked complained.

On the other hand, mountain folks also used the gun for recreational purposes. One cool, crisp fall evening I was sitting on the front porch with Daniel and his family. A full moon bathed the hills with its silvery rays. All at once the stillness of the night was broken by the voices of men and the barking of dogs. Then from out of the darkness shone lights from flashlights and miners' carbide lamps. The lights carried by the men seemed almost unnecessary for the moonlight made it seem almost like day. As the party approached the house, Daniel called out to them.

"Howdy, boys, where's ye going?"

"We's goin' huntin'."

"How long you boys goin' to stay?"

"I dunno, I reckon fer a day or two."

"Hope you boys have fun and git sump'n."

"Hope so, too."

With that brief exchange, the hunting party disappeared into the chilly night air. Daniel then turned to me to say that hunters often went back into the mountains to hunt for several days at a time. They would hunt by dawn's early light and later in the evening. The rest of the time they would play cards, take a nip or two of moonshine and sleep under a cliff or in a cave. Of course on the hunting jaunts they would carry along food and mountain spirits to imbibe. The hunting party reminded me that hunting in the mountains of southeastern Kentucky went back to the days the Shawnee Indians and other tribes had hunted in the hills of Harlan.

As the end of the school term grew near, Mary, my cute little eighth-grader, came to me one day and said her mother wanted me to stay the night with them as I returned to Sampson on a Sunday evening. Mary's family was a cut above most of the other families in the Sampson community. The children dressed better, the family seemed to have more money, their frame house looked better on the outside and apparently they ate better than my other school families. And, despite Fielding's admonition on my first afternoon in Sampson, the family was supportive throughout the school year. So I told Mary I'd be delighted to spend the night the next weekend.

The following Sunday after I had hiked across the mountain from Black Star and down into the valley, I stopped off at Mary's house, the first one I came to in Sampson. Glad to see me, they invited me in, and sat me down to as fine a fried chicken supper I have ever eaten. Skillet-fried chicken, homemade biscuits, creamy gravy, fresh vegetables, with apple pie for dessert. An outstanding meal to say the least. I gorged myself as I ate alone at the table for the family had already eaten the evening meal. When I had finished eating, we sat around the stove, talked and listened to tunes strummed on the guitar by Oscar Wilson, Mary's boyfriend. When he left, I was shown my bedroom where I retired to sleep soundly all night. (I presumed I had taken the bed of a member of the family for there were six who lived there and they did not have a spare bedroom)

Now Mary had an older sister, probably in her early twenties, who was a widow. Not as pretty as Mary I wondered later if the family was hoping that I and the sister might hit it off and do a bit of "sparkin'." In fact, since I was single, I learned throughout the year that there were several Sampson girls who possibly would have enjoyed my attention. Daniel often spoke of Charlotte, described as pretty with dark hair and dark eyes, whom he called Char-Lottie, who lived on up the mountain from him, saying she wanted to meet me. But I never met Charlotte and was hesitant to start a relationship with any other mountain girl knowing that when the school term ended, I would be leaving to return to college.

Several years later following my induction into the United States Army, I was sent to Camp Breckinridge, later a Job Corps Center, near Morganfield, Kentucky, for basic training, now that the Korean War was underway. At Camp Breckinridge, one day I bumped into Fielding. We reminisced about my days at Sampson. I learned then that time really does stand still for not much had changed since I left the remote little valley.

With the coming of the month of May, the last day of school finally arrived. The older children helped me clean the school room, pack the books and other supplies. Then they helped me carry the books down the road about a mile to a small store which also contained the Sampson Post Office. There everything was stored to await another school year, another teacher the following September. I said my goodbyes to the children and a few of the parents. As we parted I'll admit that I experienced a few tugs of the heartstrings for I had gotten attached to the school and the children during the nine months I was the teacher. Then I began my final ascent across the mountain to the Black Star Coal camp. As I passed Mary's house, I lingered to tell her mom how much I had enjoyed teaching her children. She responded with the tribute that I was the best teacher they ever had. Thanking her, I climbed the trail that would take me across the mountain.

At the Black Star mine I rode mantrip for the last time. At the Black Star Commissary, which was a beehive of activity, I caught the bus out of Pucketts Creek and at Blackmont I boarded the Greyhound bus for Pineville.

The next day I rode the bus from Pineville to Harlan. There I turned in my attendance register, grade reports and records which showed those who were promoted to the next grade. That done, I collected my last check and caught the bus back to Pineville. That summer I returned to Berea College.

I never went back to Sampson. With the exception of Fielding, I never saw anyone from that hollow again. I have always wondered what the futures of "my children" were—did they leave Sampson, what did they make of their lives? I'd like to think that I made a positive impact on the lives of the children. But, then, the traditional way of the mountain people was to go to school perhaps through the eighth grade, if that. Afterwards, the boys often followed their daddies into the mines. The girls stayed in the hollow, married perhaps a coal miner and had babies. Few changes took place since mountain folks simply just did not do anything else, perhaps did not know to do anything else. Tragic but true, because most of them were the salt of the earth—good, God-fearing, hard-working, independent, proud folk with traditional values. The people at Sampson will always hold a special place in my life. I learned many valuable lessons there. For sure it was the beginning of a rewarding career as a teacher.

Several summers ago while in Harlan, my wife ,Sue Ann, and I travelled in the area where the Sampson school had stood. What was a one-lane dirt road then was now a black-top wider road. I did not see any familiar sights but we came upon a hillside cemetery one afternoon in which we found the grave of a Fielding Hensley, probably the one I met my first day in Sampson.

II
Berea Again

Following my nascent teaching experience, I returned to the campus of Berea College for the summer session. After spending nine months in a one-room schoolhouse, I had a deeper appreciation for the teaching profession. Being away from academe for that stretch of time, however, had somewhat dulled my appetite for higher education. So I took only one course, a dry, boring economics class. Most of that summer I spent in the back of the room listening passively to the instructor while I pushed a chair occupied by a cute little redhead back and forth with my feet. Needless to say the course was a complete washout. Looking back I should have taken the summer off.

With the end of summer school, I returned to Pineville to await the beginning of the fall semester. While my third experience at Berea College was my best one, an intermediate French course proved to be quite difficult even though my instructor was a sweet French lady who did her best to pull me through the thing. Still those two semesters were just average ones so the end of the second semester found me once again back in my home town of Pineville when I secured employment at J.J. Newberry 5 and 10. Mornings were spent washing the huge plate-glass windows out front and carrying lots of heavy boxes filled with merchandise up the steep steps behind the store. In the stockroom I unpacked the boxes, checked the invoices and placed the goods on the stockroom shelves so that the counter girls could fill their baskets and restock their counters. Upon completion of those duties I was free to roam the floor downstairs, talk to the girls when they weren't busy and eat nuts and candy at the candy counter. My principal chores in the evening as closing time approached was to sweep all the floors.

It was not a bad job and I performed my tasks so efficiently that it caught the eye of Mr. Robert Lee, store manager, no relation to the General, who increased my pay and talked to me about going into a management training program. I stayed on at Newberry's during the fall semester that year while considering Mr. Lee's offer.

While at Newberry's, two rather exciting incidents broke the monotony and routinism of the days. One day the candy counter girl came up to the stockroom to replenish her supply of goodies. I was busy unpacking boxes and checking invoices when all of a sudden, she let out a blood-curdling scream from the aisle where candy was stored. I ran back to where she was; she stood in the aisle, pale-faced, shaking and pointing to an open box of candy. In the box treating itself to some of the candy was a large rat. I summoned Mr. Lee from downstairs and he and I got a large tub, filled it with water, placed the box of candy, rat and all in the water, and drowned the rodent.

On another occasion, I was assisting another one of the girls who was changing the display in one of the large front corner windows. Suddenly, we heard a loud noise which sounded like a gunshot near the courthouse square. A few seconds later a man came running down the sidewalk in front of the store carrying a revolver. The girl, who was in the window, dove for cover, as did I. Later we learned that two men, who apparently had "bad blood" between them met up on the square, an argument ensued, and they exchanged gunfire which was not all that uncommon in Pineville in those days.

Ultimately my yearning to return to college won out and I enrolled at Eastern Kentucky State College in Richmond for the second semester following my transfer from Berea College. That semester at Eastern was my best one in a while. It seemed as if I was getting back into the kind of studying it took to succeed in college.

III
Blanche

Yet when autumn rolled around, I accepted my second teaching job. By then I almost felt like a veteran teacher, having spent nine months at Sampson School. The second school at which I taught was a cut or two above Sampson. For one thing I commuted from Pineville to the Blanche School, located in the coal mining camp of the Big Jim Coal Company, just beyond Cary and Arjay on the Left Fork of Straight Creek in Bell County. That meant I was home every night sleeping in my own bed and eating from my mother's table. It also meant that I would not have to wait until the weekend to take an all-over bath. Since I still did not own a car, I rode back and forth each day with three other teachers.

The Blanche School was a three-room concrete block building perched on a hillside overlooking a stream and the Big Jim company town. Most of my students were children of coal miners. I was the principal-teacher responsible for grades five through eight. Teaching with me were two Pineville ladies who split the other four grades. I was tickled that I did not have to teach the little ones again.

Quite different from the school and community at Sampson, the students and their families were not as isolated. They could leave Big Jim, travel to the hard road and be in Pineville, the county seat, in a matter of a few minutes. Since the roads were better and since they had access to cars, weekends usually found many of them in town. Early in the school year, I learned that upon finishing the eighth grade, some students were more likely to go on to Bell County High School, located at that time in East Pineville on US 119, the road to Harlan. In fact, a sister of one of my seventh-grade girls, who visited the school on several occasions, was a Bell County High student. Like most of the students at Sampson, however, many of the kids were just not that interested in school.

Since I was principal, I was in charge of the school's entire operation, including the school grounds. For the most part, I presided over my classroom and let my two women teachers, who were veteran teachers, tend to their rooms. Every once in a great while, they would call on me to discipline a child. But since they were veteran teachers, older than myself, I did not interfere in their classrooms unless requested.

Teaching only grades five through eight, I was more satisfied with my job at Blanche. I found that I was able to get around to all their lessons just about every day. It was also exciting to be able to cover history and geography, my first loves. My students were thoroughly educated in those two subjects even though they did not get as much exposure to math and science. I also emphasized reading, spelling and English. On the whole my students were well-behaved. I do not recall having to apply the paddle more than once or twice the entire year. Generally the students were polite and courteous. On several occasions I had to break up fights on the school ground. Otherwise the school year ran rather smoothly.

In Kentucky an integral part of a school's curriculum is basketball. Someone has said basketball is a way of life, a religion in the Bluegrass State. I loved the game, grew up on it, played it. Also it became an essential part of my life at an early age. The Blanche School was located on a hill, with the playground sloping down the hill to a steep bank at the bottom of which flowed a branch or creek. Obviously the dirt and rocky terrain was not suitable for the playing of basketball. I was determined, however, to create a basketball court since two of my older boys talked about it all the time. And I sort of promised them that I would coach them to compete with teams at Arjay, just down the road, and with teams just up the road. So one afternoon after school I walked into Pineville's only sporting goods store which at that time was located in the Masonic Building on Walnut Street near the Post Office and across the street from the courthouse. The owners of the Sport Mart let me have the goals, backboards, posts and ball on credit. With the help of the boys we erected the goals and the first basketball court and team, as I recall, in the history of the Blanche School became a reality. Since my boys had to be home after school and since several worked after school, the only time for coaching and playing was at recess and lunch. Despite the drawbacks, it was not long before I began to whip a team into shape. I had a pretty good nucleus with Frank Middleton, my eighth grader, who was big for his age but, boy, could he shoot! Frank could really drill it from the outside. He would have been perfect for today's three-point shot. Under the boards, I had tall, lanky, bony Johnny Smith. Now Johnny was not a very good shooter but he could rebound and woe to anyone who made contact with his bony elbows under the basket. I am speaking from first-hand knowledge since I often scrimmaged with the guys. On more than one occasion my head came into contact with Johnny's elbows, the result of which was a rather bad headache. Then there was Harold Miller, Oakley Gambrel and Jewell Dozier to round out my top five.

On Friday afternoons we played teams located nearby and within walking distance. The men teachers worked the games as referees. Our main competition came from Tom Goodin's boys who had a nicer court because the ground was level. Many of my boys knew and hung out with Tom's boys so the rivalry was quite intense. We would walk up the road to Tom's school which was only a mile or so from Blanche. Tom would then bring his boys down to play my team at Blanche. Although I don't remember all the scores, most of the games were closely contested. Tom had better athletes but I shall never forget the day my boys took it to his on his home court. As the game ended, I still recall Tom's words, "You got me" as he tried to smile. My boys were thrilled indeed because earlier Tom's team had pasted them pretty well.

As my boys got to playing pretty well, I was looking forward to the county tournament to be played at Bell County High School. But, alas, Blanche was dealt a severe blow when I learned that Frank and Johnny, my mainstays, were too old to compete in the tournament. Being the sportsman that I am, I took my team on to the playoffs, anyway. It must have been the first time they had ever been inside a real gym for their eyes grew so large when we walked inside. Without Frank and Johnny, we did not have much of a chance. The Blanche team got bounced out in the first round by an easily forgettable score.

The disappointment my boys felt after not getting to compete in the county-wide tournament was so great that I wanted to get them a game in a gymnasium. I succeeded in scheduling a contest with the Pineville "B" team in the Pineville High School gym on a Saturday morning. At that time I was living with my parents on Laurel Street across the street from the gymnasium. I told my boys to come to the house and then we would walk across to the gym together. Saturday morning came, my boys showed up dressed in overalls, jeans, long-sleeved shirts, and wearing sneakers. We walked across the street and into the gym together. As we entered I looked at their faces as their eyes glanced around the building. What I saw reminded me of a scene from the movie *Hoosiers* when the fabled Indiana team walked into the arena for the state playoffs. My team looked scared to death. Then they saw the Pineville squad dressed out in basketball uniforms. During the warm-ups, I noticed the Pineville boys nudging each other, talking and snickering as they looked at my boys. Before the game started I told my team to forget that they were in a gym, to forget that their opponents wore uniforms while they wore overalls and just play their game.

When the game got underway, my boys were so tight and nervous that they could not hold on to the ball and they shot mostly "air balls." Just when it seemed as if they were going to get run out of the gym, they began to settle down as Frank bombed away from downtown and as Johnny cleaned the boards. Again I do not recall the final score but my boys that day shellacked the Pineville "B" team who, when they left the floor were not smiling in contrast to my kids who were beaming broadly. They never forgot the day they put it on the town team in their gym.

Since most of the Blanche kids lived near the school and because roads in the mining camp were better, the wintry weather did not take its toll on school attendance as was the case at Sampson. Most of the children made it to school except on the worst days when school was canceled by the Bell County Board of Education. Getting to the school from Pineville, however, had some suspenseful moments. Usually as the four of us rode along the few miles to Blanche conversation flowed freely. One winter morning as we left Pineville a light freezing drizzle was falling. As we made our way past Dorton's Branch and on across the Straight Creek bridge near Cary, we were in a talkative mood, mainly discussing the weather. As we crossed the railroad tracks at Cary, suddenly the car was going sideways up the road. Fortunately we were meeting no one and as Tom, who was used to maneuvering in snowy, icy weather, was trying to gain control of the car, all the talk ceased. The car was filled with silence. Momentarily Tom straightened the car and we continued our journey without incident. Tom and I talked and laughed about the episode later, remarking that for the first time in a long time, not a sound came from the back seat where the ladies were riding.

The Blanche schoolhouse was a decided improvement over the one at Sampson. My room, from which the main road through the mining camp could be seen, was large enough to accommodate the students without overcrowding. It had several windows which afforded plenty of light and was heated by a pot-bellied coal-burning stove, similar to the one at Sampson. Water was obtained from a spring and a bucket and a dipper was used. There were two outhouses adjacent to the school.

While there were these similarities, the school, which was reached by a foot bridge over the creek and a walk up the hill, never seemed as foreboding as the Sampson School. Maybe it was because there were three rooms, or maybe it was because most of the children attended school the year round, or maybe it was because the place was not so isolated so that I could spend nights at home. Whatever the reason, my experiences at Blanche were more satisfactory to me.

To help raise money to pay for the basketball goals and equipment, I decided to hold a box supper at the school. While I had never done anything like that, I soon learned that box suppers were popular in the county's schools. The box suppers of the late 1940s and early 1950s were a sharp contrast to the box lunches purchased today at Kentucky Fried Chicken. KFC boxes consist of a piece or two of chicken, a roll, potatoes and gravy. Box suppers at the schools were full meal deals. Of course, there was always fried chicken, but then there were the candied sweet potatoes, corn-on-the-cob, butter beans, potato salad, dressed eggs, made-from-scratch biscuits, and for dessert, homemade apple pies made from dried-on-the-porch apples and made-from-scratch yellow cake with chocolate icing. In other words, the box suppers at the schools came not from cans nor boxes nor from the kitchens of Betty Crocker. No, they were monuments of good old down-home country cooking, the kind I grew up on.

The box suppers were prepared by either the older girls or their mothers. On the night of the event they were brought to school where they were auctioned off. The highest bidder bought a box and a side attraction was getting to share its contents with either the girl or her mother who had prepared it. Usually box suppers were a substantial money raiser for the schools.

When I announced the box supper, I invited the children and their parents. I also requested the girls, or perhaps their mothers, to fix the boxes to be sold. Prior to the evening on which the box supper was scheduled, I learned that there might be attempts to disrupt the proceedings by some local older youths as well as some fellows from surrounding communities. Not waiting to find out how reliable the reports were, I passed the word to my students who apparently spread the message around the area. I also procured the services of a deputy sheriff as security for the evening.

The box supper turned out to be the one where no one came. There were no disturbances, attendance was sparse. Only a handful of people showed up. The local school board member was the evening's auctioneer. My mother fixed a delicious box and accompanied me to the school. It was auctioned as the only box sold that evening. The box supper was a dismal failure. I have often thought that my strictness regarding behavior at the event may have caused many to stay away. I was so disappointed at the low turnout that I did not attempt another box supper. As it turned out, I paid for the playground equipment out of my own pocket. It was worth it since the children got such a kick out of playing roundball on the rocky, sloping, hillside court. And they played the year around except on rainy, snowy days. Windy days did not stop them. They simply allowed for windage when they put up a shot. Believe me, they got pretty good at shooting the ball when the wind was blowing hard.

The school year at Blanche passed rather quickly. Since I did not stay in the community, I was not involved in the lives of the students and their parents like I was at Sampson. School days became rather routine with few exciting incidents to enliven the time. Of course, I taught only the upper grades and had little contact with the children in the other two rooms. I was still single and soon noticed that some of the older sisters of my students came to school, apparently to check me out. Maxine Miller, a seventh grader, came to school one day when Bell County High School was not in session. In my early twenties at the time, Maxine was probably 16 or 17 and somewhat attractive. But I did not pursue her. I had another student, Eaf Hooker, who also had an older sister. Dark-haired and buxom, Mary, Eaf's sister, came to school one day just to visit. I thought perhaps that she just wanted to see what the new man teacher looked like. I did not mind visitors as long as there was no trouble. But the Hooker woman did not attract me either. Maybe it was her name—Hooker—that scared me off. As at Sampson, I decided to avoid getting involved with any of the local belles. Maybe that is why I remained single so long.

The experience I gained at Blanche as principal-teacher was both valuable and fulfilling for me. Growing up and living in Pineville, I found that I related quite nicely to children out in the county. It was also good that I could teach in a mining camp where practically all the kids were either coal miner's sons or coal miner's daughters. The mines, the camps, the company towns and stores, the families of coal miners and the demographics of the coal-producing region attracted me. When I later got to the University of Kentucky in Lexington, it was natural for me to purse as a research interest coal mining, miners and their unions.

One thing I learned teaching in that kind of environment was that the people were God-fearing, that they were proud to be Americans, that they were intensely patriotic and nationalistic. Never was there a thought given to whether there should be Bible readings and prayer to start each school day. It was assumed that the teacher would just do those things. Also it was taken for granted that every morning students would stand and recite the Pledge of Allegiance to the flag. It did not enter my mind nor the minds of the children that someone would be offended by this daily ritual. While teaching in those days, I did not dream that the Ten Commandments would be banned from classroom walls across the state.

This is not to say that all the kids came from Christian homes. Of course there were the usual sins of the mountain people—drinking to excess, carousing, gambling, shootings, murders, moonshining—the bottom line was that mountain folk loved their country and feared God. They had a deep respect for the church even though their lives were not always Christ-like. It was normal and accepted that school teachers inculcate traditional values into the children. Like the Puritans of old, mountain people cherished Biblical teachings, although they often broke its commandments.

When the school year ended, I turned in all my reports at the offices of the Bell County Board of Education which at that time was located on the first floor of the Bell County Courthouse overlooking Kentucky Avenue. In fact, it was a common sight in those days to see the County School Superintendent and some of the office staff make the daily trek across the street (Kentucky Avenue) for coffee at Morgan's drugstore. More often than not Superintendent Bill Slusher could be observed sitting in a chair looking out an open window, which fronted Kentucky Avenue, on warm, sunny days.

There was no attention paid to a no-smoking policy in the late 1940s. So when I walked in the courthouse and down its tiled corridor to the Board of Education offices, the atmosphere was that of a bluish haze as a cloud of smoke filled the air. In the corners of the hallways sat the ever-present cuspidors which were the targets of tobacco chewers of which there were an abundance. I wasn't in the courthouse very often but when I was there and left, my clothes reeked of tobacco smoke which only washing or cleaning could erase. My father, after lengthy days in the courthouse and its two or three courtrooms, often came home smelling of tobacco smoke and with a headache. Nobody at that time paid any attention to the "second-hand" smoke issue being addressed today. My father, who found it necessary to be in the courthouse almost every day, never smoked nor drank. Today he would be a leading advocate of "smoke-free" government buildings.

IV
Blue Collar Days—
Pennington Gap, VA

After my teaching stint at Blanche, I remained in Pineville for the summer. I did not return to J.J. Newberry where I had worked earlier. Instead I took a job with the R.C. Gambrel Construction Company headed by a friend of my father. During the three-month span, June through August, I worked at helping set power poles for a power line across one of Harlan County's steepest hills, helping to build a power substation at Pennington Gap, Virginia and in a coal tipple on Straight Creek.

To set the power poles, I first had to climb the steep hill. Upon reaching its summit, I had to help dig holes for the poles. By the end of the day's work, I was dog-tired. Happy was I to get home, take an all-over bath, eat supper, although I was nearly too tired to eat some evenings and fall into bed for a night of sleep which seemed way too short. Early the next morning the routine of the previous day resumed.

With the completion of the power line project, the next job found me just across the mountain from Harlan working on a power substation job at Pennington Gap, Virginia. Lasting several weeks, that job was not as physically exhausting. Days were spent at the substation, evenings found me wandering down to the local pool hall. Since I did not shoot pool, the main attraction for me was the big board out front which bore major league baseball scores. So I watched the scoreboard to see how my favorite team, the St. Louis Cardinals, were doing. Afterwards I walked back up to the street to the old hotel where I stayed during the week. The main attraction inside the hotel parlor was a marathon checkers game played by several of the local checkers addicts. One old bespectacled gentleman seemed to be the champion. I do not recall anyone ever beating the old guy.

Following my hiatus in Pennington Gap, I was assigned to a job shoveling coal in an old coal tipple in Bell County's Straight Creek section. Since I still did not own a car, each morning I boarded the bus for the ride to my job. I spent the day shoveling coal. At noon I stopped to eat the brown bag lunch prepared by my mother. After an afternoon in the coal tipple, I knocked off around five o'clock to catch the bus back into town. More than once some real-life coal miners, covered with coal dust, were on the bus. As I boarded I was regarded with curious stares since I, too, was smeared with coal dust although it was obvious I was not a miner.

And so the summer passed rather routinely. The days, which commenced just after day light, ended early in the evenings as a weary young man climbed into the sack soon after supper. The three months of strenuous blue-collar labor taught me some valuable lessons. In the first place it came to me that I did not want to spend my life as a laborer. Secondly, days spent alongside the blue-collar class gave me a deeper appreciation for the rank-and-file working men and women who made and still are the nucleus of modern industrialized America. It dawned on me that summer that coal miners deserve everything they get for going into the bowels of the earth to produce the coal that helps run America's industrial machines and power plants.

V
Hillary

With my blue-collar days behind me, the cooler days of autumn found me once again in the school room. An air of uncertainty and tension hung over the entire nation that fall following the outbreak of America's forgotten war in Korea which began when the North Koreans invaded South Korea by crossing the 38th Parallel. The Korean conflict ushered in the draft which made it necessary for young men like me to go to the local draft board in Pineville to register. As the war increased in intensity it became more apparent that my official "greetings" from the President of the United States would soon arrive at Box 144 in Pineville. At any rate I began the school year in a one-room schoolhouse located at Hillary in Bell County. To get to Hillary, I traveled out US 25 E, the main road from Pineville to Middlesboro. At the foot of Log Mountain, I turned off on what used to be Kentucky 74 which took me to the coal mining camp of the Southern Mining Company at Colmar. From Colmar I continued on to Hutch on the hard road. Leaving the tiny community of Hutch, site of a school building made from creek rocks, I made my way along a one-lane dirt road, fairly level in places and winding and hilly in other places. From Hutch to Hillary I soon sensed that I was headed back to the boondocks. The road was narrow, houses were further apart, the terrain was uneven, here and their gardens were separated from the road by rail and wire fences.

Having no automobile it was essential that I board during the week in the community where I was teaching, meaning that once again there would be no all-over baths until the weekend. In contrast to the Sampson community, however, my boarding place at Hillary was predetermined. It seemed that a man named Hillary Hoskins (I don't know whether that was where the school derived its name) and his wife, a friendly couple in their 60s, always took in the teacher. Their nice, comfortable, one-story white farmhouse stood at the end of a lane about fifty yards or so from the road. Since they had no children at home, I had a nice bedroom with double bed all to myself. They had their own bedroom, there was a good-size living room and the kitchen was large enough for cooking and eating. The Hoskins had a well for water but since there was no indoor plumbing, I had to trek to the outhouse to relieve myself. At night I took a "potty" or "slop jar" to my room which I emptied the next morning.

The Hoskins' household was heated by a coal stove around which we sat evenings after supper. In contrast to evenings spent in Daniel's home at Sampson, there was more conversation and less listening to programs like the "Suppertime Frolic." The fact is that Hillary and his wife, both in quality of life and in education, were a cut above Daniel and his family. Hillary's homestead was larger and better furnished. And the fare served by the woman of the house had greater variety since Hillary, who was retired, tended a nice vegetable garden adjacent to the house. Being a country-farmer, Hillary was always looking for ways to supplement home-grown veggies. One morning he hurried into he house to fetch his shotgun. As he went out the back door he explained that several wild ducks had lit on the pond near the house. In a few moments I heard a loud blast from the shotgun. A short while later a beaming Hillary walked in carrying a pair of ducks. That evening for supper we enjoyed succulent breast of duck, my first, and a tasty treat indeed.

Getting to and from the Hillary School was accomplished in much the same manner as my trips to and from Sampson except there were no mountains to climb and no man-trips to ride. In fact, most of the Hillary parents farmed and I always suspected that a bit of moonshine was carried on in the neighborhood. My father usually drove me out to Hutch on Sundays, sometimes on Monday morning, where I got out to walk the dirt road two or three miles to Hillary. On Friday afternoon, he usually met me at Hutch. One Friday he got tied up in court so I hiked from Hutch to

Highway 25 E to catch the bus into Pineville. By the time I had traveled that distance of several miles, it was almost dark. So there I stood on the highway waiting on the Greyhound. Suddenly the bus sped around a curve so fast I guess the driver failed to see me. Fortunately a man named Herbert Hoskins, who was related to Hillary, came along, recognized me, stopped and gave me a lift into town.

Unlike my experience at Sampson, I did not get snowed in at Hillary. One weekend a heavy snow blanketed the hills and valleys of Bell County. I was determined to get to school on Monday since most of my children walked. Apparently the county system did not have snow days at that time for I rode the bus to Middlesboro, hired a taxi to take me to Hillary. Up Cumberland Mountain we went slipping and sliding as I held my breath. Near the top of the hill we turned off onto Dark Ridge Road. Following that winding, narrow road we blazed a trail through the newly-fallen snow. The taxi driver, accustomed to traveling snow-covered roads, made the trip without incident as we became the first vehicle to travel the road to Hillary that morning. As we approached the school the kids looked out to see who dared be out in the snow. As we passed house after house I waved to them and soon after I got to school and started the fire in the old pot-bellied stove, they began arriving. Perhaps we were the only school in session that wintry day in Bell County.

The Hillary schoolhouse, like the one at Sampson, was heated by the burning of coal. As principal-teacher, I was chief fire builder. Cool, clean water from a mountain spring was brought by students to the schoolhouse. The children used a dipper to pour water into cups for drinking. Behind the school were the two omnipresent outhouses. The building sat beneath a clump of trees near the road. The terrain surrounding the school was strewn with rocks and boulders, making it unfit for a playground. There was no adjacent pasture for the playing of football so the common game played by the pupils and their teacher was once again Antney-over. We had a lot of fun playing that game and the children never seemed to tire of it. Across the road from the school was another grove of trees and land which sloped down to a fairly level rock-free surface, affording the children a place to toss a ball back and forth. Those ball games and occasional hikes through the woods and hills following trails familiar to the pupils were the only forms of recreation at Hillary School. When snow covered the ground there were always snowball fights as the students took great delight in throwing at their teacher.

Grades one through eight made up my school room at Hillary. My eighth-grade girl, Faye Robbins, was a very smart intelligent girl who probably continued her education at Bell County High School. There were two seventh graders, a girl and a boy, both mature for their years. Charlene Hill, my seventh-grade girl, came to school every day and helped some with the little ones upon completion of her work. J.C. Barnett, my seventh-grade boy, was a strapping, athletic type who was not all that interested in school. He was attracted to Charlene but she did not return his attention toward her. J.C. did participate in the softball throw at the county-wide field day at Bell County High School. The other pupils were in grades one through six. Again I did the best I could trying to teach all eight grades in one room. Spelling, reading and arithmetic were covered daily to all pupils and as time permitted I worked in geography and history in the upper grades.

For the most part the students were well-behaved, polite and did not "sass" their teacher. I had a paddle but do not recall ever having to use it at Hillary. Most of the children seemed to be more into school evidenced by the fact that they attended regularly even on bad days. The homes from which most came and the parents they had reflected a little better upbringing. While somewhat isolated, they could be on the hard road in a matter of minutes. From there they could easily reach either Pineville or Middlesboro for shopping.

Aside from the usual schoolroom activity each day, the students and I enjoyed some wonderful hikes together. They knew the trails through the woods, so off we went on pretty autumn afternoons. Having grown up in the mountains of southeastern Kentucky, I enjoyed walks in the woods especially in autumn when the sun shone brightly, when cool weather had turned the leaves into reds, golds and oranges, when the sky overhead was azure blue. It was a delight then for my pupils to take me on a hike. Since I was principal-teacher, I would cancel afternoon classes so that we could take nature walks through the beautiful countryside, a hands-on kind of science lesson. Sometimes the trail led us across steep places but they enjoyed it and to me it was exhilarating. Many years later after I had received my Ph.D. from the University of Kentucky and had gone to Augusta College in Georgia to teach, I brought my college students to Kentucky on a four-day field trip. A central feature of those excursions was a predawn hike up the Tri-States trail at Cumberland Gap. My, they hated to get up while it was still dark outside. We drove from Middlesboro up the mountain to the parking area and by flashlight started our ascent up the trail. By the time we reached the summit and the marker indicating the merger of Kentucky, Tennessee and Virginia, day was beginning to dawn so we watched a gorgeous sunrise in the east. The students along with my wife and myself enjoyed those hikes which were climaxed by the group standing on the outline of the Commonwealth of Kentucky to sing "My Old Kentucky Home." Afterwards we retraced our way back into Middlesboro where we sat down to a hot country breakfast.

My days at Hillary were numbered because during the days of late autumn I received a notice from the Pineville Draft Board to report for a preinduction physical. When I related this news to my Hillary children they were disappointed and saddened that I would be unable to complete the school term. In fact, two of my girls, Charlene and her half-sister Faye Helton, walked with me on my last day at school before Christmas vacation to the little store at Hutch where I waited on my father. That may have been because Charlene, an attractive girl with dark brown hair, dark brown eyes and dark complexion, seemed to have a school girl crush on her teacher. When I told her goodbye for the last time, I noticed that she was misty-eyed. I never saw nor heard from her nor from any of my kids at Hillary again.

Before Christmas break I was visited by Mr. Warren Robbins and Mrs. Beulah Pursiful from the county office. They surprised me one day by coming unannounced for a visit. All the time I was at Sampson no one from the county office came to see me. Although I had not expected them, the school room was in good shape and the pupils were in order at work at their desks. For about an hour or so, Mr. Robbins and Mrs. Pursiful observed me and the children, talked to me and to them, asked if there was anything we needed. My response was that outside of a decent playground, I could not think of anything. Before they left, they "treated" the children to Christmas candy and fruit. It goes without saying that all of the children clutched their "treats" as if they had just discovered a sizable treasure.

I learned that day the school board had found a replacement for the remainder of the term. So at Christmas break, I waited for induction orders from Uncle Sam at the Pineville home of my parents.

VI
You're in the Army Now

I shall never forget my last night at home before leaving for a two-year stint in the United States Army. Usually I can eat. In fact, all my life I've had a ravenous appetite. But that evening, as I sat around the table with my dad and mom, not knowing whether I would ever see them again, I got so choked up that I had to leave the table. And I never finished the delicious meal prepared by my mother. That night was a restless one for me and the next morning once again I could scarcely eat. When the time came for our goodbyes, I hugged and clung to my mom and dad as tears flooded my eyes and washed my cheeks. Of course, like the good parents they were, both tried to assure me that all would be well if I kept faith in the Lord. Promising them that they could count on that, I walked to the Greyhound bus station in Pineville to catch the bus to Corbin.

At Corbin in the old Wilbur Hotel, I, along with a number of other draftees, was given a superficial physical examination. Then we were sworn in and told to go outside and board the bus for Fort Knox, Kentucky. On the way out the door one of the draftees ran smack into a screen door. Called back a re-examination disclosed that he had severely crossed eyes. Why, he had not even seen the door! Once sworn in, however, you just do not get sworn out! So he rode the bus with the rest and sat around at Fort Knox for several days until orders came for his discharge.

At Fort Knox I was given a GI haircut which meant that after thirty seconds or so in the barber's chair I was a "skin head." Then off to the quartermaster I went where I was issued Army fatigues, khaki shorts and tee shirts, socks and combat boots. I was now in the Army!

About that time a chilling incident which almost unnerved me took place. I was called into a separate room and asked, "What the hell are you trying to pull?" When I answered that I did not know what they were talking about, the sergeant exclaimed, "You know damn well what I'm talking about." It seemed that another "Paul Taylor" had taken a basic Army literacy test and flunked the thing, perhaps in an attempt to get out of the Army. And they thought I was that "Paul Taylor." So they made me retake the test which was so simple, somewhat like a GED examination, that I answered every question correctly. The fact was I had never taken nor seen the test until they requested that I "retake" it. And when I scored 100 percent, they were sure I was trying to pull a fast one. There I was, alone and innocent in a small cubicle while they were trying to decide my fate. After what seemed like an eternity, an Army NCO came in to advise that it would be in my best interest never to try anything like that again.

My time at Fort Knox was short-lived. Soon I was on a Greyhound bus headed for Camp Breckinridge, near Morganfield, Union County. There I was introduced into sixteen weeks of basic infantry training. The rumor was that after a sixteen-week cycle, my outfit from the "Screaming Eagles" of the 101st Airborne would ship out to Korea.

Now I never made it to Korea. About halfway through basic training during what was one of Kentucky's worst winters, for example, we were out on bivouac, sleeping in pup tents, in sub-zero weather. One day while the company was out on a twenty-mile march with full field pack, the company clerk roared up in the company jeep. After a brief consultation with the commanding officer, he yelled out two names, mine and a fellow from Somerset named Billy Joe Anderson, to report back to the company to ship out. My heart was in my throat as I climbed into the jeep for the trip back to the post. On the way the company clerk turned to inquire, "Who do you fellows know in Washington?"

Astonished, Billy Joe and I exchanged glances, shook our heads, and responded, "No one."

The company clerk rejoined, "Well, orders just came down from Washington transferring you both to an artillery outfit on the other side of the post." As it turned out, recruits in the artillery outfit, which was about halfway through an eight-week cycle of basic training, were assigned to other stateside bases. Billy Joe and I were sent to Fort Sam Houston, Texas for training as Army medics. I never knew why I was suddenly transferred from the infantry to the artillery at Camp Breckinridge. I suspected that my father, who was a good friend of our Ninth District Congressman, James S. Golden, had something to do with it. He never told me, I never asked him.

Upon completion of the medical training at Fort Sam Houston in San Antonio, Texas, I was assigned to the Army hospital at Fort George G. Meade, Maryland. At Fort Meade I spent the remaining eighteen months of my two-year hitch working in hospital supply. When my company commander learned that I had just about completed college, he suggested that I give weekly troop information and education lectures on topics chosen by the Army to the nurses, WACS and various hospital personnel. The topics were propaganda for the most part but it felt good to be "teaching" again. I must confess, however, that most of my "students" knew much more about some of the topics than I, a lowly PFC, knew.

Time spent at Fort Sam Houston and Fort Meade, aside from military duty, was rewarding. Being at Fort Sam, as it was commonly called, gave me opportunity to immerse myself in the history of San Antonio and the southwest. On weekends I visited the Alamo, where Davy Crockett, Jim Bowie and Colonel William B. Travis, of Saluda County, South Carolina perished. Of special interest were the large cavities in the historic mission-fortress caused by the terrific bombardment during the siege of 1836. While in San Antonio, several of my GI buddies and I enjoyed the city's scenic river walk as well as the Mexican portion of the old city.

Fort Meade, located midway between Baltimore and Washington, afforded opportunities to visit both those old cities. My favorite was Washington where I toured most of the historic sites of the nation's capital. Especially awesome was a tour of the Pentagon on a weekend when the halls and building appeared to be deserted. One evening near midnight as I strolled down a long, wide corridor of Washington's old Union Station, I met Massachusetts Senator John F. Kennedy face to face. In Baltimore the old row houses fascinated me. On Saturdays I went to College Park, Maryland to watch the University of Maryland Terrapins, coached by Big Jim Tatum, play. My Army days in both Texas and

Maryland gave me opportunity to experience a good deal of the history I had talked about in the classroom.

My days at Fort Meade were spent in various ways. In addition to the weekly lectures and my work in hospital supply, I was able on occasion to slip off to the hospital lounge to watch the televised McCarthy Committee hearings. One day one of the civilian employees and I were in the lounge watching the proceedings when we were supposed to be working. All at once our boss, a chief warrant officer, loomed up in the doorway, obviously looking for us. I slumped down in my seat to escape detection. The civilian was not so lucky. He was spotted, summoned and reprimanded by our superior.

I also got to make several ambulance runs. On one occasion, I and the ambulance driver dispatched a young psycho, in strait jacket, to the Walter Reed Army Hospital in Washington. Another time, on a stormy night, I went on a run to a small house in Glen Burnie, Maryland, where the driver and I took a stretcher up a narrow, winding staircase to pick up an Army wife who was already in labor. Fortunately for us, we got her to the Fort Meade Hospital before she delivered.

While at Fort Meade, I encountered a GI named Paul Ralph whom I had known at Fort Sam Houston. In fact one day at Fort Sam I went to the PX for ice cream. While there, my company was called to formation and a roll call took place. I would have been AWOL had not Paul Ralph answered for me. Months later Paul had gone AWOL and was in the brig. One morning he was assigned to me at the Army hospital at Fort Meade for detail. When we met face to face I remembered how he had saved me from being AWOL at Fort Sam Houston. I did not have the heart that day to impose hard labor on him. In essence he had the day off!

On January 10, 1953, my two-year enlistment period was up. Following my discharge, I entrained for Pineville. Down through historic Virginia and the beautiful Shenandoah Valley I traveled on the Norfolk and Western Railway, one of the country's last railroads using steam-driven locomotives. In fact, I made many trips back and forth from Washington to Knoxville on the N&W during my one-and-one-half year stay at Fort Meade. At Knoxville, my parents nearly always met me for the drive to Pineville as they did that last time on January 11, 1953.

VII
Eastern

My discharge in early January was opportune for it afforded me the opportunity in late January to enroll at Eastern Kentucky State Teachers College (now Eastern Kentucky University) to finish my degree. Actually, this was my second sojourn at Eastern. Prior to my two-year tour of duty in the United States Army I spent the second semester, 1948 to 1949, in Richmond where I continued pursuit of the B.A. degree. That semester I lived in the quadrangle in one of the dorms on the third floor. Occupying a suite on the first floor was Charles A. (Bull) Keith, former major league baseball player and then a social studies teacher at Eastern. The dorm room in which I lived was one of a suite of four rooms occupied by other Eastern male students. My roommates were Hugh Shyrock, who liked to party on the weekends, Lawrence Grimaldi, who was some sort of a ladies' man, and Alfred Bianchi, who enjoyed both coeds and sports.

One morning while we were getting ready for class my radio was tuned to the popular Mimi Chandler radio show on WVLK, Lexington. Mimi always began her show by playing "On the Sunny Side of the Street." One of the guys decided to turn up the volume to nearly an ear-splitting sound. In a few moments, "Bull" Keith stood in the doorway of our suite, remonstrating us with the words. "What in the ding blast is going on in here?" With that, Keith marched over, unplugged my radio and retreated downstairs.

I turned to Hugh Shyrock and remarked, "See, I told you guys to keep the volume down." Shyrock answered for me not to worry, that he would retrieve my radio. Once the radio was back in its place, we kept the volume down from then on.

I had an average semester at Eastern that year. Among my professors were Saul Hounchell, L.G. Kennamer, Virgil Burns, Jonathan Truman Dorris, and Keith. Kennamer's geography class came just before lunch. As soon as class ended we headed out to Bales Restaurant on East Main near the railroad tracks for a delicious lunch. Bales was a popular eatery for both Eastern students and Richmond townspeople in those days.

Spring afternoons were spent watching the Eastern baseball team, coached by Turkey Hughes, play on a diamond located behind one of the old Model High School classroom buildings. When we weren't watching Eastern, we used to play a bit ourselves. One day a foul ball careened into and broke a window in the Model building. Shortly J. Dorland Coates charged from the building and gave us sand lotters a real tongue lashing.

Being at Eastern that semester gave me a chance to renew acquaintance with a buddy I had known at Berea. Billy Hiatt, from the Wildie community in Rockcastle County, and I got together frequently, mainly to discuss sports, especially baseball. Billy's roommate was his brother, Jack. Billy Hiatt now is the owner and operator of Hiatt's 5 & 10 in downtown Mt. Vernon.

The semester at Eastern passed rather quickly. Unlike Berea College, Eastern did not have as many restrictions on its students. In the late 1940s Eastern was somewhat of a party school, a reputation that continued for many years. And it was also a "suitcase" school, that is, when the weekends came most students left the campus on Friday afternoon to return on Sunday evening.

With my army days behind me, I naturally returned to Eastern for the second semester, 1952 to 1953. I now had the GI Bill of Rights which helped defray my expense and my army experience had matured me for academics. Instead of returning to the dorm, I acquired a room on Oak Street, just off Lancaster Avenue and a few blocks from the campus. Needing only one semester to complete my B.A. degree in the social science area, I buckled down to going to class every day (early on, especially at Berea I cut classes to play basketball, etc.) and to the kind of serious studying that had not been part of my schedule earlier. Finally I became the student I should have been. The fact is I was somewhat of a late "bloomer." My professors at Eastern that semester included Harvey LaFuze, Virgil Burns, William D. Ward and Tom Samuels. The course under Samuels was a Public Hygiene and Safety course. When Samuels did not meet the class, Virginia Durbin of Lexington, Miss Popularity at Eastern in 1954 and a Miss Eastern candidate in 1955, took over the class.

My second semester at Eastern passed quickly and uneventfully. Living off campus I did not become involved in dorm life and campus activities that had occupied my student days earlier. I went to class, studied in the library, ate in the cafeteria and for recreation, watched the Eastern Maroons, coached by Paul McBrayer and led by Bob Mulcahy, who now lives in the Andover Forest area of Lexington, and Tom Holbrook. Sophomores Jack Adams and Ron Pellegrinon were also members of the 1953 to 1954 Eastern squad. Not having a car, when I chose not to eat in the cafeteria, I strolled several blocks down to Main Street and ate either at Brandy's Kitchen or at Doc Ferrell's near the Madison County Courthouse.

In May 1953, after my most successful semester since entering Berea College in 1944, I received the B.A. degree in social sciences from Eastern. On hand to witness the historic occasion were my parents, my brother John and my sister Emma. Following the commencement ceremony in Brock Auditorium, we drove to Cincinnati, along US 25, to visit my father's sister and husband, Mr. and Mrs. Tom Warman. Then I took the summer off to prepare myself for entering graduate school in the fall at the University of Kentucky to pursue a Master's degree in United States History.

VIII
The University of Kentucky

Late August, 1953, found me in Lexington at the University of Kentucky where I had enrolled as a graduate student. My aim was to achieve a Master's degree in United States history which was my first love. Chairman of the History Department at UK was Dr. Thomas D. Clark, now Kentucky's historian laureate. The faculty was equally outstanding. Clement Eaton, a pre-eminent historian and scholar of the ante-bellum South, James F. Hopkins, one of the editors of the Henry Clay papers for many years, and Bennett H. Wall, who was an authority of recent United States history, were three of my mentors. Aspiring graduate students and colleagues of mine included Mac Coffman, a military historian who taught at the University of Wisconsin-Madison, for many years, John E. Wilz, who taught at the University of Indiana-Bloomington, Leonard P. Curry, who had a lengthy tenure at University of Louisville, Monroe Billington, who went west to the University of New Mexico, and Holman Hamilton, already an author of a two-volume biography of Zachary Taylor, and a journalist who was a Ph.D. candidate.

Graduate school days were spent attending lecture classes, usually in the morning, and seminars in the afternoon in Frazee Hall. When not in class, we were growing roots in the old Margaret I. King Library where we had cubicles in the stacks. On one occasion we secured a large study room on the top floor of the library. Noontime found us journeying out to the Chef Sear's restaurant on Nicholasville Road where we consumed delicious lunches at reasonable prices. Breakfasts and evening meals were eaten in the cafeteria located on the ground floor of the Student Union. My main diversion in autumn came in watching the UK Wildcats football games which were played at old Stoll Field on Euclid Avenue where the Singletary Center now stands. Coaching the Wildcats was Paul "Bear" Bryant who presided over the most successful UK football program to date. While the "Bear" had a highly successful team at UK, his principal nemesis was the Tennessee Volunteers whom he finally defeated at Stoll Field in 1953. The '53 Wildcats were captained by Ray Correll of Somerset and Tommy Adkins of Corbin.

Across the street from Stoll Field Adolph Rupp and the basketball Wildcats played to packed houses. Cold winter nights found me inside Memorial Coliseum watching the Cats pound visiting teams. After the game, I would make my way to courtside to listen to Coach Rupp's famous post-game interviews conducted in his inimitable style. Following the Wildcats in 1953 to 1954 was a real treat since they were undefeated with a 25-0 record and led by All-Americans and Hall of Famers Cliff Hagan and Frank Ramsey. The 1954-55 season was marked by a Wildcat defeat that I shall never forget. On January 8, 1955 the Cats lost to Georgia Tech by a score of 59-58, a shocking upset that ended their all-time home winning streak at 129 games. Following that game I, along with most fans, sat in my seat in stunned silence.

Since basketball was and is my favorite team sport, I forsook my graduate school history colleagues in March to wander over to Memorial Coliseum to watch the "Greatest Show on Earth," the Sweet Sixteen competition in the boys high school state championship. From Wednesday night to Saturday evening, I took in all the games. And I saw some outstanding games and players featuring Ralph Carlisle's Lafayette Generals and Hazard's John Cox who later became an All-American at UK. Naturally, I took a lot of ribbing from my history buddies for disappearing to engage in a hedonistic lifestyle those four days.

In one of my most interesting seminars, I chose as a topic for a seminar paper, "A History of the Coal Industry in Southeastern Kentucky," beginning with the discovery of coal near Middlesboro by Virginia land surveyor Dr. Thomas Walker and his companions as they passed through Cumberland Gap and entered Kentucky in 1750. That paper, which was well received by my professors, whetted my appetite for my Master's thesis, "The Coal Mine War in Harlan County, Kentucky, 1931 to 1932," a conflict which was triggered by the famous Battle of Evarts, May 5, 1931.

Two years of graduate study, including summers, spent in seminars, lecture courses and the all-important French foreign language examination, led to the completion of the Master's degree in history in May 1955. Graduate school was both challenging and satisfying. Since I loved history so much, I thoroughly enjoyed my professors, most of whom were nationally known and respected and the less formal chat sessions in the library and at lunch with my fellow graduate students. A special highlight of the informal talks we had was listening to Holman Hamilton, who was working on his doctorate at the time, regale us with historical anecdotes and stories. When I was back at UK working on my doctorate, it was my good fortune to sit in Dr. Hamilton's class on the Middle Period in United States history. Hamilton not only possessed a thorough knowledge of that period, but he enlivened his lectures with stories, a technique that I emulated when I taught that same course at Augusta College. The Hamilton technique became with revisions the Taylor technique which many of my students copied in their teaching and classes.

One humorous incident which I shall always remember occurred during Holman Hamilton's class in the Middle Period in United States history. The class, which included more undergraduate than graduate students, took place just before lunch. Hamilton, who was an excellent lecturer, had a habit of walking back and forth in the front of the room as he lectured, all the while keeping an eye on the class from the front to the back of the room. Apparently, he noticed one day that a coed seated between two guys was smiling about the same time every day. After this had gone on for some time, Hamilton's curiosity finally got the best of him. So one day as the girl was exiting the room, he called to her to inquire what was humorous for he had checked himself to see if he had said anything that induced smiles. The young lady hesitated before saying that about the same time every day her tummy rumbled which caused both her and the two fellows to smile. Being the personable gentleman that he was,

Hamilton smiled as he told the attractive coed that he was glad to have the mystery solved because it seemingly annoyed him.

My closest friend at UK in those days was John Wilz, who was a journalism major before deciding to pursue graduate study in history. Although a Hoosier, John and I had a number of things in common. Both of us were very religious, John was a devout Catholic, I was a faithful Methodist who attended First Methodist Church on West High Street where Adolphus Gilliam was pastor. (Rev. Gilliam's brother, Will, was a history professor at UK for a number of years.) John and I were both rabid St. Louis Cardinals baseball fans during the days when Harry Caray was the inimitable voice of the Cards. John and I both loved country music and we loved history. So we'd meet at the Student Union cafeteria for breakfast most mornings and John was instrumental in me joining the US Army Reserves in Lexington.

John was dating a young woman named Susan Stark, from Louisville, who had a twin sister named Ellen. I met Ellen through John so we double-dated quite a lot. We sat in Stoll Field on a cold, snowy day to watch UK play Vandy. Afterwards we went to the North Lime Grill to eat. On one occasion we went to Renfro Valley to take in the Barn Dance. Another time the four of us joined a number of other history graduate students for a picnic at Natural Bridge State Park. One Sunday evening the girls' aunt, who was a sorority housemother, entertained us with dinner at the Phoenix Hotel. Another Sunday we all went to Louisville to visit the girls' parents.

Ellen, who was staying in a white house with a big porch on South Broadway near the Coach House, and I studied together quite a lot and attended movies at the Strand and Kentucky Theaters downtown on Main Street. Since I did not have a car, I usually walked from where Ellen lived to where I was staying on McDowell Street in Chevy Chase. (Mrs. Sawin, who also attended First Methodist, was a widow who lived alone and she let me have an upstairs bedroom for raking leaves and shoveling snow.) One night after Ellen and I arrived where she was staying, I sat off on the long walk to Chevy Chase. Along the way a thunderstorm moved in, soaking me to the bone before I reached McDowell Street.

Ellen and I got along really well and had some good times together.

But since she was a devout Catholic and I was a strong Methodist, she and her folks thought it would never work if our relationship was consummated. After several months of intense courtship, we went our separate ways. Meanwhile, John and Susan were married, John became a history professor at IU—Bloomington, and they became parents of eight children. Years later, in failing health, John was gracious enough to help me get my doctoral dissertation into publishable form. He passed away a couple of years ago in Bloomington. In 1990 the University Press of America published *Bloody Harlan*, a revision of my Ph.D. thesis.

While most of my grad school friends stayed on at UK to work on the doctorate in history, with the conferring of the M.A. degree in May 1955, I left Lexington, returned to Pineville for the summer and began a search for a teaching position which led me back to Georgia and to high school.

IX
Tucker

Upon completion of the Master's program, I acquired my first high school teaching position. That appointment turned up in a most unusual way. In 1955 the State of Georgia was paying its teachers considerably more than the Commonwealth of Kentucky. So on a summer trip to Georgia to visit relatives, I stopped off to make inquiry at the DeKalb County Board of Education in Decatur, Georgia. Following my return to Pineville, a call from DeKalb County came offering me a position as high school social studies teacher at Tucker High School. Without an interview and without laying eyes on the school I accepted the job over the phone. By September 1955 I was in Georgia to begin what turned out to be a four-year tenure at Tucker High.

Since I still did not own a car, I, along with the Tucker High principal, James F. Goolsby, set out to secure housing for myself in Tucker, at that time a rural bedroom community a few miles from Decatur, Georgia and Atlanta, Georgia. (Today Tucker is part of the sprawling metropolitan Atlanta complex) One day as we visited a home in the Tucker community, a large dog from an adjoining yard came charging across the yard headed straight at me. It happened so suddenly that I did not have time to get scared. Fortunately the cur did not bite me but just about tore one pants leg off. Incensed, the principal took me to a men's store in Decatur and outfitted me with a brand new suit. Needless to say, the bill for the suit was dispatched to the dog's owner, whose children I had in class that semester.

Unable to find a place to stay in Tucker, I finally located a one-bedroom apartment on Church Street in Decatur, about a block from DeKalb County Courthouse. The first few weeks of school I rode the Greyhound bus back and forth to Tucker since the tiny community was located on the main highway to Athens, Georgia, site of the University of Georgia. Waiting on the bus got to be quite a hassle. Eventually I was able to hook onto a ride with three teachers who rented a house in Decatur near the Emory University campus. All three taught at Tucker. One was women's basketball coach and physical education teacher at the high school. The other two were at the elementary school. Since I was still single, those early morning and mid-afternoon rides back and forth to school were reasonably pleasant, except that none of the three was a "looker." I finally became somewhat interested in one of the elementary teachers who was the best looking. But, alas, one of my high school colleagues had already begun a relationship with her. So I was content with bachelorhood for the moment even though several of the high school girls seemingly had crushes on the teacher they called "Tall Paul." In fact, at the 1990 Tucker High School reunion, several of the ladies from that era confessed to my wife that they had crushes on me in those days. In contrast to modern times, however, a student-teacher relationship in the 1950s beyond the normal classroom scenario was quite uncommon to say the least.

While at Tucker for four years, I got involved with the students as much as possible. Since I was a sports fanatic, I attended most of the football and basketball games. Most Friday nights found me on the sidelines cheering on the Tucker Tigers. During basketball season I was the official scorer in addition to refereeing a few women's games.

At Tucker I received my first taste of coaching. And for two or three years I coached the eighth grade boys in football, basketball and baseball. As a teacher, part of my philosophy was getting to know my students as much as possible beyond the structured and more formal classroom situation. Coaching afforded me the opportunity to do so. The students always appreciated my showing an interest in them by coaching them as well as attending their games and functions.

My teams were reasonably successful. I've always felt like my boys would have won more games if Tucker, a class B school then, was not always going up against much larger schools like Decatur High and Southwest DeKalb High. My basketball coaching included what surely must be an all-time oddity and a record of sorts although I have not checked into it. One afternoon my "little" Tucker eighth graders played the much bigger and more talented Southwest DeKalb basketball team. Being from Kentucky, I liked the fast-break up-tempo style of offense employed by the late Adolph Rupp and Rick Pitino. That day I knew if I used that strategy my boys would get killed. So I told my team that once they got the ball, give it to Robert Carter, who was a pretty good dribbler and shooter. As instructed, they gave it to Robert who spent most of the game dribbling and faking. When he got a wide-open shot, he took it. My gamble paid off. The Southwest DeKalb team became so confused that it threw them off their game so that they could not even make a wide-open shot. Final score: Tucker 14, Southwest DeKalb 0. Yes, I had coached a shutout in basketball, which has to be one for the ages.

At Tucker High I also sponsored the school's safety patrol. In 1955 high school safety patrolmen were traffic guards at school crossings. They've since been replaced by traffic guards, most of whom are women. As patrol sponsor, I got to take a memorable trip to Washington, D.C. and to New York City, my first visit to the "Big Apple." The trip was made by train which was anything but boring. In New York City, a trip to the top of the Empire State Building, the nation's tallest at that time, and to the Statue of Liberty were particularly impressive.

Another trip I recall with fondness was escorting my home room to Callaway Gardens, a famous attraction in the southwest corner of Georgia. Since I was now the proud owner of a 1956 green and white Ford Fairlane, I drove. My passengers were several of the high school girls. We had a great time on that trip as enroute, one of my colleagues, a Mrs. Thompson and I took turns passing each other at speeds well above the posted limits. Fortunately, we did not get apprehended by the Georgia State Patrol and both of us got our students home safe and sound. While both of us conducted ourselves rather foolishly on that trip, the news that two Tucker teachers used a state highway as some sort of a NASCAR racetrack on that class trip became legendary in the corridors of Tucker High.

In Georgia in the late 1950s school desegregation became a hot issue. In those days most Georgians preferred to maintain a dual school system. While Tucker was an all-white suburban neighborhood, places like Decatur and Atlanta had large black populations. Already Virginia, in defiance of the 1954 Brown v. Topeka Supreme Court decision, had closed its public schools. It appeared that Georgia was moving in the same direction, meaning that I, along with thousands of other public school teachers, might join the ranks of the unemployed. While Georgia never did adopt the Virginia plan, I did not wait around to see what might happen.

X
GMA

One Sunday while scouring the classifieds of the *Atlanta Journal-Constitution*, I noticed a small ad seeking a secondary social studies teacher. When I responded to the advertisement, I found that the school was Georgia Military Academy, now Woodward Academy, a private military school for boys, located in College Park, Georgia. Following an interview, I was offered a position at GMA. After four fun-filled years at Tucker High, I resigned to teach in a military school where I became known as Captain Taylor.

For four years, 1959 to 1963, Captain Taylor taught social studies at the Georgia Military Academy. During that four-year span, the Academy's student body consisted of several hundred cadets including Greg and Tim Barker, the twin sons of Susan Hayward and actor Lex Barker, who played Tarzan on the silver screen. It figured that both Greg and Tim were excellent swimmers who anchored the Academy's swim team. Among the cadets were Bobby and Herman Talmadge, Jr., the sons of former Georgia Senator Herman Eugene Talmadge, the grandsons of four-time Georgia governor Gene Talmadge. The student body also included Cadet Philip Gramm, who became and only recently retired as a United States Senator from Texas. Gramm was also a former Republican Presidential candidate.

GMA was a decent place to teach. As Captain Taylor, I wore a military uniform and cap, complete with the insignia of a captain, to class every day. In contrast to Tucker High where periodically I had to send disruptive students to the office with the words, "get your books and get out." Military discipline was the order of the day at GMA. If a cadet broke one of the rules, was insubordinate or guilty of misbehavior, he would be placed on report and dealt with by the commandant. If the offense was serious enough, such as the time one of the cadets sneaked beer into the dormitory at homecoming, demotion in rank or expulsion was ordered. Less serious offenses carried a penalty of extra detail or suspension of weekend passes to go home. At GMA, then, I could teach and not concern myself with discipline.

Each morning and every class period, the ranking cadet marched the students into class. After they were all in the room, standing at their desks, the cadet turned to me, offered a snappy salute as he spoke, "Cadets reporting for instruction in World history, sir." After I returned the salute, he then completed a left face or a right face, as he gave the order, "seats." Each class began in that manner. At the end of class the cadets were ordered to their feet and marched out of the room.

At GMA, as at Tucker High, I attended most of the basketball and football games. While I did no coaching, I became good friends with the men's basketball coach, Joe Stanley, from Indiana who was a hoops fanatic like myself. The men's coach designated me official scorer for the men's varsity games. At the end of the year, at the awards banquet, I received a certificate awarding me a GMA varsity letter as official scorekeeper.

As scorer, I made most of the road trips with the team. One of the most memorable was a trip to Pine Log, Georgia in north Georgia where the GMA lads played the local team in a gymnasium reminiscent of the movie *Hoosiers*. Most of the spectators for the home team, clad in homespun garb, watched the game from primitive stands. A few overalled gentlemen stood over in a corner by a pot-bellied stove. The gym ceiling was low. While the Pine Log team was accustomed to shooting shots with a low trajectory, the GMA team unused to playing in such an environment and unable to compensate for the low ceilings, lost the game.

During my four-year sojourn at GMA, as at Tucker, most summers were spent returning to Kentucky to take courses leading to the doctorate in history at the University of Kentucky. Some summers I rented a room in Lexington on East Maxwell Street near the UK campus. (The house in which I stayed had a "rooms" sign out front and was operated by a gracious elderly couple. Today the house, in more of a run-down condition, appears to be some sort of a rooming house) In the summer of 1960, I decided to take a room in the same house in which my brother, John, stayed in Richmond and commuted back and forth to Lexington. That summer my brother and I ate breakfast and supper at a local Richmond eatery known as the Golden Rule Café. One of the morning waitresses was Charlotte Sutton who had an older sister named Sue Ann. My brother, who had become acquainted with Charlotte before I arrived on the scene, introduced me when I began eating at the Golden Rule. Through my brother, John, and Charlotte, a blind date was arranged between myself and Sue Ann. In the summer of 1960 she and I had our first date. A year later on June 4, 1961 we were married in Richmond's First Baptist Church by my father, who was a licensed local Methodist minister. Sue Ann joined me in East Point, Georgia for my last two years at GMA. On April 27, 1962, our son, Larry Floyd, was born at Piedmont Hospital in Atlanta, Georgia.

I remained at GMA through the summer of 1963. One summer I worked as a telephone salesman for an outfit in Atlanta. That was quite an experience but with a family, extra income to supplement my teacher's salary came in handy. Basically my job consisted of calling individuals, including corporate executives, and asking them to buy tickets to various events, such as the circus and baseball games. From all the tickets I was able to peddle, the gentleman who ran the organization gave me a right handsome cut. With a wife and baby boy at home, the job helped pay the bills while affording extras like trips to McDonald's.

After spending four years at GMA, in 1963 I decided to return to Lexington to pursue full-time work on my doctorate in history. The decision was not entirely my own. In fact my wife and I had made plans to purchase and move into our first home in the Riverdale section of Clayton County, Georgia. Those plans were short-circuited when the administration at GMA assessed the faculty for contributions to the school's development fund. Gifts were not voluntary and confidential.

Faculty were expected to contribute a certain, definite amount. With a new wife and baby, I did not feel that I could give what the school expected. Subsequently, my loyalty to the institution was questioned. I was called into an administrator's office where I was told that my services to the school were no longer needed, the first and only time in my life I was fired from a job.

XI
UK—Revisited

Upon my return to UK and Lexington in autumn 1963, my wife, our 18-month-old son and I moved into a one-bedroom apartment in Cooperstown. We lived in D building which was located across the street from several fraternity houses. Living in Cooperstown enabled me to walk through the area where the William T. Young library now stands to reach the campus, Frazee Hall where my classes and seminars took place, and Margaret I. King library where I studied and engaged in research. Behind the Cooperstown apartment building where we lived were basketball courts where we observed U.K. All-American Pat Riley and his girlfriend "playing" basketball one afternoon.

My grad school colleagues from the mid-1950s were all gone, having finished their degrees and having acquired faculty positions in various colleges and universities in the midwest and elsewhere. The outstanding UK history faculty was still in place—Dr. Thomas D. Clark, Chairman, Dr. James F. Hopkins, Dr. Bennett Wall, along with Dr. Carl Cone and Dr. Enno Kraehe who had come to UK while I was away.

Beginning in 1963, days were spent taking courses leading to the doctorate in history in Frazee Hall. When I was not in class, I was in my cubicle in the library reading, studying and working on seminar papers. Since I lived just a few blocks from campus, I walked home to lunch with my wife and our son. After lunch, it was back to the library for the afternoon. In those days it was necessary for history grad students to "grow roots" in the library as one of the professors put it. Nights were spent at home playing with our son until his bedtime, watching TV, and attending UK basketball games, our principal diversion at that time. When my wife and I attended games, we left our son with a grandmotherly type named Mrs. Marcum who lived on Oldham Avenue. And wouldn't you know it? Although our son lived in Lexington for four years while his dad was in grad school and was exposed to Wildcat basketball, he became a University of Louisville fan, which he still is, as he grew up.

When attending basketball games at Memorial Coliseum, my wife and I lined up with UK undergrads to get better seats for the games. And, more often than not, we took deviled ham sandwiches to eat since we went early to watch the freshmen play. The succulent odor of the sandwiches attracted many a glance from the undergrads as we ate them.

One of my biggest hurdles on the road to the doctorate was passing two foreign language exams. Since I had taken two years of French at Berea College, I chose French for the first exam. Right before that examination, our son became quite ill and it became necessary for us to admit him to Good Samaritan Hospital. Despite the strain of our son's illness on my wife and myself, which required us to be at the hospital most of the time, I decided to go ahead and try the French exam. While I did not pass, exposure to the test gave me a good idea of what to expect and the second time I took it, I successfully cleared that hurdle.

Passing the German examination was an entirely different matter. I had not taken any German courses so I had to start from scratch, learning the vocabulary and learning how to read German. Eventually, I enrolled in a German class tailored principally for graduate students. I attended class in the morning and in the evenings, my wife gave out German vocabulary to me. This crash course in German enabled me to pass my second language requirement for the Ph.D. in history.

During my second tenure at UK, 1963 to 1967, it became necessary for Sue Ann to gain employment in order to help defray expenses. Familiarity with furniture and carpeting led her to Stewart's Department Store on Main Street in downtown Lexington where she worked several nights a week under the supervision of Mrs. Virginia Lindsey, who was a hard-nosed overseer, but who eventually became a good friend. (On visits to

Lexington after I had taken a position at Augusta College in Augusta, Georgia, we would go by to visit Mrs. Lindsey in her retirement.) On nights Sue Ann worked, I would feed and bathe our son, and at nine o'clock, we would go pick up my wife and Mrs. Lindsey whom we would take home on our way to Cooperstown. Once we arrived back at our apartment, I would treat Sue Ann with homemade brownies which I had thrown together while she worked.

We enjoyed our days at Cooperstown since it was close to the campus. The University, however, decided that the complex would be ideal housing for single students. The married students vehemently voiced our protests but to no avail. We were ordered to evacuate Cooperstown, so we moved to a basement apartment on Kees Road, owned by the late Rex Martin, builder of "The Castle" on Versailles Road, off North Broadway behind what is now the Legends baseball stadium. That move made it necessary for me to drive back and forth to UK and go through the daily hassle of finding a parking place close to the campus. We spent our last two years in Lexington, 1965 to 1967, on Kees Road where we shopped at a Winn-Dixie and at a Begley's Drug Store in the Northland Shopping Center. Our son, Larry, got his hair cut in a barber shop in the shopping center and on pretty spring and summer evenings, we would push Larry in his stroller to a Dairy Queen on North Broadway, just up a block from Loudon Avenue.

Meanwhile, I continued course work and seminars preparing myself for the Ph.D. qualifying exams. Those exams were both written and oral, and the written part commanded three entire weeks. The prelims, as they were called by graduate students, were not easy, requiring an expansive knowledge of United States history, European history, history of the British Empire and a minor field in political science. Also required was an in-depth knowledge of bibliography relating to the five fields. After successfully passing the writtens, the orals took place on April 27, 1967, which was also Larry's birthday. Since the examination was scheduled for the evening of the 27th, we celebrated Larry's birthday during the day at Jerry's, at the corner of North Broadway and New Circle Road where a Shell station now stands. The celebration went well until the waitresses gathered around to sing "Happy Birthday." At that point Larry slid as far down as possible without falling out of the high chair.

While I was back at UK the second time, Dr. Thomas D. Clark, Kentucky's Historian Laureate, asked me to become his grading assistant for his Kentucky history course. That semester, Clark taught the course in the courtroom of Lafferty Hall which housed UK's College of Law. My duties consisted of attending the lectures, taking the attendance roll, and grading all the examination papers. I received compensation for these duties, but had I not, it would have been worth my time just to sit in on the class and hear Dr. Clark's lectures. While attending the class, I sat in the jury box.

One morning as Dr. Clark lectured, a guy sitting near me fell into deep slumber. I watched the fellow, wondering what Dr. Clark would do when he noticed him. And I want to say little escaped Clark's attention in the classroom. Finally, Dr. Clark looked over and saw the fellow. He stopped, called my name, telling me to rouse the student from sleep. I reached over, shook the guy several times before he regained consciousness. Dr. Clark, without missing a beat, told the drowsy fellow to get up, go get a cup of caffeine and return to class the next time it met. I can't recall that man ever lapsing into sleep in Clark's class again.

Another morning in the springtime of the year while Dr. Clark was teaching, the UK lawn mower crew decided to mow the grass outside Lafferty Hall. Since the courtroom lacked air-conditioning, the classroom windows were open. The clatter of the mowers, while not drowning out the lecture completely, made it almost impossible for students to hear. Exasperated, Clark stopped, turned to me and told me to go outside and quiet the mowers. Not knowing what to expect, I got up, strode out of the room, confronted the crew and told them to quit mowing the grass while class was in session. To my surprise, they cut off the mowers and I returned to the classroom.

Upon completion of the Ph.D. qualifying examinations, the summer of 1967 was spend in research for my doctoral dissertation. I also traveled to Augusta, Georgia to interview for a position on the history faculty at Augusta College. I learned of that opening through a graduate school colleague, John DeBerry, who had been for an interview but decided not to take the job. The interview went well, I was hired and late summer

1967, found my wife, Larry and myself packing our belongings and hiring Spangler movers of Middlesboro to move us from the Horse Capital of the World to the Golf Capital of the World where I began teaching in autumn, 1967.

During my first two years at Augusta College, 1967 to 1969, I engaged in the research and writing of my Ph.D. dissertation, "Coal and Conflict: The United Mine Workers of America in Harlan County, Kentucky 1931 to 1941." Upon completion of my dissertation, I defended it in Frazee Hall in May 1969, during a time of unrest at the University because of the Vietnam conflict. I received my doctorate in history in May 1969 while Dr. A.D. Kirwan was acting president of the University.

XII
Augusta College

I wanted to stay in Kentucky and teach but there were few opportunities. My department chairman, Dr. Thomas D. Clark, even made a phone call in an attempt to get me a job at Murray State. Finally I landed at Augusta College, a four-year liberal arts institution in Augusta, Georgia, home of the famous Masters Golf Tournament. So in September 1967, I began a twenty-seven year career as a college history instructor from 1967 to my retirement in 1994. I taught college freshmen, sophomores, juniors, seniors and graduate students all about United States history. In addition to teaching the two college survey courses, the United States to 1877 and the United States from 1865 to the Present, I also taught upper-level courses: The Age of Jackson, the Civil War and Reconstruction, the United States from 1789 to 1850, The Old South, the New South, the United States from 1877 to the present and the British-Empire-Commonwealth. I also added to the curriculum two upper-level courses which were quite popular: the History of American Labor and the History of American Sports. On the graduate level I offered: Special Topics in American Social History and Appalachian Studies.

At Augusta I was known as a non-nonsense instructor. For example, I expected students to be in class every day and to be on time to class. If a student was late, my favorite motto was: "Be reminded, this class begins at 10:00, not 10:01 or 10:02." Needless to say, once a student received such a reminder, rarely was she or he ever late to class again. I even had a few students, like Jeff Hays, who ran all the way across campus to avoid the "be reminded." A few who got there late simply would not enter so that they would not "be reminded." And I must say that my formula worked for most of my students made it to class on time.

I was also known as a strict professor, some said hard, because I set high standards for myself as well as my students. I expected the students to write legible, intelligible essays, using good grammar and correct spelling of words. If they did not do this, they received a copious quantity of vermillion ink on essay examinations and research papers. They referred to that as the "Taylor treatment." Then there was the "Taylor technique" which included my pacing back and forth in front of the class using arm and hand gestures as I lectured enthusiastically about Sam Houston, Daniel Boone, John L. Lewis, Ty Cobb and others. The students told me that several copied the "Taylor technique" and demonstrated for their peers before I entered the classroom. And I must say that, according to reports, those few brave souls did an excellent job of mimicry, even to voice diction and inflection. My son, who finally decided to take a couple of my courses, said he didn't realize that I was such a performer, in a sense, an actor. I loved history, was excited about the discipline, used an up-beat tempo in the classroom. The students grew to love it and passed the word to their friends to "take Taylor" so that my classes were always among the first to fill up during pre-registration.

Despite being known during my first years as a "hard," "stern," college professor who rarely smiled, in time I began to mellow. My students, some of whom were afraid of me at first, realized I cared about them. They knew I was a good listener whose office door was always open to them. I had many chats with students about their courses, of course, but also about a number of other things, including sports, religion and politics. With regard to the latter two topics, they realized I was a conservative, albeit a Christian, and that I was not interested in being politically correct in the classroom. For several years I was campus advisor to the College Republicans and for the Navigators, Campus Crusade for Christ and InterVarsity. My students knew, too, that I could relate to them on a one-on-one basis and that they could seek advice from me on non-academic matters and personal concerns. In short, I was known as a friend to students as well as a teacher at Augusta College. Since my retirement in 1994, I have kept in touch with a number of former students at Augusta

College. And I must have attended over two dozen weddings to which students invited my wife and myself.

In July, 2004, Rhonda Howard honored me by requesting that I read the scripture in her wedding to Edward Marschalk at Trinity-on-the-Hill United Methodist Church in Augusta.

A good number became public and private school teachers imitating the Taylor technique. Among that group were Della Carter, Nancy Foss, Helen Mulholland, Chris Lane, David Hollingsworth, now at UK working on his Ph.D. in history, Jesse Gordon, Rhonda Howard, Ricky Peace, and Herman Ross.

At Augusta, teaching was the main emphasis. I loved to teach and took my teaching seriously. Rarely did I miss a class. The exceptions came when I was too ill to walk or get out of bed to meet my students. When the prestigious Masters Golf Tournament hit Augusta in April every year, I met every scheduled class even though many of my colleagues dismissed class to go to the golf course. Most of my students cooperated nicely and came to class during Masters Week when practically everything else in Augusta, including public and private schools, were closed. As an added attraction during the Masters Classic, I let my students predict the winner and the winning score of the golf classic. The student who either picked the champion and total score correctly or who came the closest, received five bonus points which was added to his or her final grade.

In addition to the Masters, I also let students predict baseball divisional champions, World Series winners, as well as the winner of the NCAA Division I Championship in basketball. In my Sports History classes, I let the students participate in a class pool in the Kentucky Derby, described as "The Greatest Two Minutes in Sports," and the Preakness Stakes. The students got into the pools for one dollar each and usually split the pot.

As an added incentive for students to attend class and to be in class on time, at the end of the quarter, I gave those "perfect" students five bonus points every quarter. I had a good number of students who received bonus points for perfect attendance and getting to class on time.

As in my high school teaching days, I got involved in the college athletic program. Attending nearly every men's basketball game from the day I set foot on campus, as the years passed I began attending the women's basketball, volleyball and softball games. I made many road trips following the men's and women's teams. Usually, as the occasion arose, I enjoyed a post-game meal with the teams. As a result of this type of camaraderie with the students, many regarded me as a friend and if I missed a game, they quickly picked upon my absence. The students really appreciated my presence, coming up to me after games to thank me for coming and more often than not hugging me and my wife.

As a faculty member who was interested in the athletes and the athletic program, I was appointed to the College Athletic Committee a number of times. As a new member I, at first, did not raise questions regarding the budget and student athletic fees. When it dawned on me that the Committee was mainly a "rubber stamp" outfit for the Athletic Director, Marvin Vanover, who grew up and attended the old Hall High School in Harlan County, I became concerned. So questions began to flow from my mouth as I assumed the role of trying to protect the interests of the students. In short, I went to bat for them. Apparently student athletic fees were raised arbitrarily at the whim of the Athletic Director and endorsed by the Committee. Although my stand was unpopular with the Committee, I was successful in getting one proposed increase put before the students in a referendum. Once it was voted down, future increases were ram-rodded through the Committee with little or no input from the students.

I also plugged into trying to get increased funding for the women's athletic programs. On this issue I went head-to-head with the Athletic Director who, opposed to the increase, accused me of having ulterior motives as we got into a shouting match. Relentlessly, I pressed the matter and finally, the Athletic Committee, in an unprecedented move, voted extra money for the women's basketball, volleyball and softball teams which were still funded far below the men's teams. But in the days before gender equity in college athletics became a hot topic with the NCAA, I felt a deep sense of pride in my accomplishment at Augusta. As part of my campaign to get more money for women's athletics, I also published two articles in *The Bell Ringer*, the school newspaper, supporting the increased funding. While the Athletic Director and his successor, Clint Bryant, got upset and refused to speak to me, my efforts in behalf of the women's athletic program were met by a deep sense of gratitude from the women's coaches as well as the teams. They now knew that they had a real friend on the College Athletic Committee. Despite being severely under-funded compared to the men's programs, the women's athletes were, on the whole, more successful on the court, on the field and in the classroom. Athletic Director Vanover was friendly and invited me to athletic banquets and parties before our differences. Afterwards he crossed me off his list. I became somewhat of a persona non grata around the Athletic Director's office and department.

To enhance my students' education, I began in the early 1980s to take my upper level classes, made up of history majors and minors, on field trips. Traveling in private automobiles led by their teacher, my Civil War students and I hit the road to Charleston, South Carolina for a boat ride across scenic Charleston Harbor to tour Fort Sumter where the Civil War began. On the way to Charleston, the class stopped at Miller's Bread Basket, a Mennonite restaurant in Blackville, South Carolina, which was featured on ABC's *Good Morning America* several years ago, for a full country breakfast consisting of eggs, bacon, sausage patties, grits and delicious homemade bread. My History of the Old South classes toured several of Charleston's lovely antebellum homes, gardens, churches and cemeteries. We also visited the gravesite of John C. Calhoun, one of South Carolina's great statesman in the first half of the nineteenth century. Among the homes toured were the Joseph Manigault House, the Nathaniel Russell House, which featured a free-standing stairway all the way to the third floor, the Aiken-Rhett Mansion, the Calhoun Mansion, the Edmonston-Alston House near the Battery, and the John Rutledge House. A panoramic view of Charleston Harbour with Fort Sumter in the distance was observed. We felt as if we had stepped back into history as we recalled Charlestonians watching the attack of Fort Sumter at dawn on April 12, 1861.

My Sports History classes enjoyed an Atlanta Braves baseball game in Atlanta, Georgia, the first major professional sporting event for many of them. And a New South class visited Kannapolis, North Carolina where we toured a high-tech Fieldcrest-Cannon textile operation. There we saw cotton fiber spun into thread and into sheeting for the bedrooms of America. We went down into the cold, dark dungeon of a deep mine that was known as Mary Helen mine.

The "mother of all trips," however, was the excursion to the coal mines of Harlan County, Kentucky with my Labor History classes. A four-day trip, we went down into the cold, dark dungeon of a deep mine that what was known as the Mary Helen Mine in the 1930s. By the 1980s the Mary Helen Commissary was still standing and in operation but the mine was operated variously as Bow Valley, Great Western and New Horizon. Dressed as coal miners, we descended underground as far as two miles where we saw coal being mined by a continuous miner which was operated by a single man. We also saw a roof bolter who, with a helper, inserted bolts three feet long into the roof to help hold the mine's top into place. We saw coal passed from the continuous miner to a conveyor belt to a multi-story washer to a coal train at the foot of the mountain. There it was pulled out of the hills of Harlan by a diesel locomotive and transported to utility companies in Georgia and South Carolina. My students and I were given samples of coal to take back to Georgia as well as samples of another famous Kentucky product variously known as "white lightening" or "moonshine." We also got to talk to modern-day coal miners, men and women, about labor problems, working conditions and the quality of life among coal mining families.

On these trips to Kentucky, my students and I also visited several surface mining operations. We watched as bulldozers and monster trucks removed dirt to get at coal seventy-five feet below the earth's surface. Once the coal was obtained, huge draglines filled in a monstrous cavity and the restorative process began. But once "stripping" of the coal was done, the mountains were scarred permanently.

By the 1980s, the decade when I first began taking students to Harlan County, once virulent UMWA territory, was mostly non-union. A younger generation of coal miners saw no need for the union for which their father and grandfathers had valiantly fought. Several of these third- and fourth-generation miners related that they had better working conditions, safer places in which to work, and better fringe benefits than they would have received had they belonged to the union. But nearly all of the current crop of coal miners agreed that their improved lifestyles and working conditions had come about because of the union.

My classes learned much from these trips. When they returned to campus, they told their friends what they had experienced. Ultimately acquaintances of the students who made those field trips with me showed up in my classes. My philosophy of teaching history encompassed the experiential in the field as well as verbalization in the classroom. We went, we saw, we learned.

Not content with letting my students tour the coal country, several classes were treated to a trip to Lexington and the Bluegrass. In the "Athens of the West," we toured Henry Clay's Ashland and the Hunt-Morgan House. Mixing pleasure with education, my students got the chance to go to Keeneland where one fellow, on his first trip to the track, more than made up for his trip expenses at the betting windows. That student kept his winning formula to himself so that his teacher and his colleagues were far less lucky than he. One class visited Claiborne Farm near Paris, Kentucky where Forty-Niner and Ferdinand were showcased and where Secretariat is buried. Several classes went to Commonwealth Stadium with their teacher to see the UK Wildcats play.

On the return trip to Georgia, we stopped by the Jarrett House, a restored Victorian country inn, in Dillsboro, North Carolina for an all-you-can-eat country dinner. The menu featured fried chicken, country ham, baked ham, fresh mountain trout, homemade biscuits, buttered potatoes, green beans, candied applies, pickled beets, coleslaw and fruit cobblers. While my appetite was legendary around campus, on one of the trips, Gene Collins, "out-ate" his teacher. None of my students never forgot the "mother of all trips." Each one was a topic of conversation long after we returned to campus.

On the different field trips made by my Labor History students to Harlan County, several incidents, which were amusing later but somewhat harrowing at the time, took place. In 1982 on a tour of the area, the group and I happened on a drive-in movie theater on a Friday night just as cars and pickups were turning in to watch the picture or "pitcher" show. That night the marquee out front advertised "To Kill or Be Killed." Now before the trip to Harlan, my class was fully informed about the history of "Bloody Harlan" and its high incidence of murder. Upon seeing the name of the Friday night movie, Nancy Foss, one of my students, asked to stop so she could go across the road to snap a picture of the marquee. Just as she got poised to shoot the snapshot, a pickup, turning into the drive-in, back-fired very loudly, one of the loudest I had ever heard. My student photographer jumped off the ground, came running back across the road yelling, "Oh, Dr. Taylor, I've been shot, I've been shot." So shaken was she about the incident, she forgot all about taking the picture.

On another occasion, while traveling around the county with a different class, we spied a house on a hillside with a washing machine and "washing" hanging on the front porch. The outward appearance of the frame dwelling presented a classic case of poverty in Appalachia. Again a request for a picture was made. We parked on the side of the road, barely off the pavement, overlooking Clover Fork. As the students got ready to take a photograph, suddenly a young man, probably in his twenties, came charging out on the porch, yelling at us. When a woman appeared in the doorway, he turned to scream, "Get me my _____." Obviously, we did not wait for the completion of that sentence as we jumped into our vehicles and sped away.

On yet another sojourn into Harlan County, my students and I visited the historic Harlan County Courthouse where shootings had taken place in the hallways. That day we decided to peek into the happenings in an upstairs courtroom. Once inside we sat on benches in the rear to listen to proceedings which involved one of Appalachia's favorite pastimes, "moonshining." Suddenly the door to the courtroom opened and in stepped a hulk of a mountain man, all bearded and overalled. As he sat down on an adjacent bench, Russell Lohrman, one of my students, all the color drained from his face, leaned over to whisper, "Dr. Taylor, that man sure looks mean." Now while growing up in the area I had seen many similar looking men, it was a first for my students. So when I suggested leaving the "mean-looking" man behind in the courtroom, they were more than ready to join me.

Another time, on a visit to Evarts, where the famous "Battle of Evarts" took place on May 5, 1931, we parked our cars on Main Street to get out for a walking tour of the little mountain community. While strolling around the town, we noticed that the local police car had parked nearby, apparently to keep us under surveillance since our automobiles bore out-of-state license plates. Finishing our walk, we got back in our cars and headed up Clover Fork to view Harlan's one-time premier mining area. As we traveled along, we soon noticed that we were being "tailed" by the police. Careful to obey all local speed limits and traffic laws, the "tailing" lasted for a few miles and a few minutes before we were left alone to continue our wanderings.

My students, on the trips to Kentucky, always found out that their teacher was human after all. Since I grew up and had taught in the county, I always had said that I knew the area like the "back of my hand." On one dense, foggy morning those words came back to haunt me. As a cavalcade of a dozen vehicles, with myself in the lead car, made its way up Highway 421 on the way to the old, historic Mary Helen Mine at Coalgood, known then as New Horizon, I turned off on a narrow, one-lane road which I believed would take us to the mine. Now I had traveled that route many times before but that morning the fog was extremely dense. No sooner had I left the highway when I realized that this road did not take us to Mary Helen. But it was too late for behind me was a string of traffic with lights penetrating the dense fog. I had to keep going. Finally the road dead-ended at a small frame house. A mountain woman came out on her porch to look at the strange procession of vehicles which had invaded her peaceful, foggy hollow. While she watched, I turned around in just enough room without hitting her house and in turn, the cars following did the same. One fellow in one of those elongated pickups, while experiencing considerable difficulty, got his vehicle turned around barely missing the house. The caravan then crept slowly back down the narrow road to the highway. And while all that was going on, Rhonda Howard, the designated class photographer who was riding in a car with a sunroof, was standing up in the front seat, busily snapping a picture of the traffic jam caused by her teacher for posterity.

On these class trips to Kentucky, my students were always poised with cameras and on one occasion with a videocam to get a picture of their teacher in action. So I had to be extremely careful not to make a misstep along the way. In other words, I had to be perfect. Such was not the case on the last trip before my retirement. (In addition to the tour of Harlan County coal mines, I tried to expose my students to additional historical scenarios in the hills. One class toured the Lincoln Museum, funded by

Colonel Harland Sanders who gave Kentucky Fried Chicken to the world, which is located on the campus of Lincoln Memorial University, at Harrogate, Tennessee, just beyond historic Cumberland Gap. Also visited was the Colonel Sanders Museum which includes a number of original artifacts from the Colonel's original restaurant where Kentucky Fried Chicken was born at Corbin, Kentucky. We also motored to the summit of the Pinnacle located in Cumberland Gap National Historic Park for an excellent view of the Cumberland Gap. On that trip while visiting the tiny town of Cumberland Gap, Tennessee, several students and myself decided to explore a nearby bubbling mountain stream. Now, as a young lad growing up in Pineville, I had great fun playing in creeks and making my way from one bank to the other across slippery rocks. That day in Cumberland Gap I was not so lucky. Venturing down into the brook, I was just about to get set to take a picture of some of my students who were playing in the cool water, when all of a sudden my foot slipped on one of those slippery, moss-covered rocks and down I went, camera and all. Embarrassingly, I got up, shook the water from my camera, brushed myself off and with water dripping from my sneakers and pants legs, climbed up the bank to dry ground. Luckily, I tumbled into the water so fast that my students did not have time to take a picture of their fallen teacher in the creek. But several came rushing over to ask, "Dr. Taylor, are you hurt? Are you all right?" Assuring them that I was okay, I cautioned them against relating what they had observed to my wife who was elsewhere with other students.

All the class trips were fun as well as educational. While most of my students had never visited Kentucky, a few had never been outside the state of Georgia. And it was always very rewarding and satisfying to help them expand their minds to experience first-hand things we had talked about in the classroom.

After twenty-seven years of teaching college students at Augusta College, my teaching career, which began in that tiny one-room schoolhouse deep in the hills of Harlan and spanned almost half a century, interrupted by schooling and military service, came to a pleasant end with my retirement in June 1993. I returned to teach part-time at Augusta from January to June 1994.

As I neared my retirement, my students planned and put on a retirement roast in my honor which took place on May 28, 1993 in the dining room of the College Activities Center on the Augusta College campus. One hundred students, and a sprinkling of college staff and administrators, attended the affair which featured liberal servings of the famous Sconyers Barbecue and all the trimmings made popular during the Carter Presidency when the same menu was served at the White House. The students, along with presenting their favorite professor with several nice gifts, regaled the audience with anecdotes, mostly humorous, about experiences with their teacher both inside and outside the classroom. At the conclusion of the gala, most of the students came forward to shake hands, hug and have pictures made with their mentor. Fittingly the warm evening rang down the curtain on the long and enjoyable career of a man who truly was born to teach.

XIII
Reflections

From the one-room schoolhouse at Sampson in the hills of Harlan, to the three-room schoolhouse in the Blanche coal camp, to the Hillary School in remote Bell County, to the halls of Tucker High in DeKalb County, Georgia, to the campus of Georgia Military Academy in College Park, Georgia, to the historical campus of Augusta College in Augusta, Georgia, my teaching career spanned an era from the mid-1940s to the mid-1990s. During that time, I had the wonderful privilege of teaching little ones how to read and spell. I'd like to think that I got them started on a learning experience that would last a lifetime. The older boys and girls who knew how to read and spell learned how to "figure" as arithmetic was called in the Kentucky mountains in the mid-1940s. As time allowed a bit of geography and history was thrown at the children as well as a dose of physical education.

From my first day in the tiny classroom at Sampson I cared for my students. And I did not stop caring until I bowed out of the classroom in 1993 to 1994. I cared that they learn, of course, but my caring attitude went far beyond the classroom. It mattered greatly to me that they would improve to make a good life for themselves, one superior to that of their homes and parents. I wanted them to succeed in the classroom but more importantly to succeed in life. While I cannot account for what happened to those pupils I taught in the one-room and three-room schoolhouses, I saw first hand that many of the students I taught at Tucker High in Georgia had done quite well for themselves when I attended a 1990

Tucker reunion. For example: Charles Bannister, a strapping Tucker High School football lineman, was elected to Georgia's General Assembly. Many of the girls, Lois Oliver (Alexander) Glenda Guffin (Banister), Jo Ann Whitaker, Judy Parrish, Beverly Wood and Linda Carver, were married, had families and were career women. The years had been kind to a number of students I taught in the mid to late 1950s.

The students I taught at Augusta College were successful also. A good number became public and private school teachers, imitating the Taylor technique. Others became successful in business and professions like law, nursing and the ministry. Seeing these students grow, mature and carve out a niche in society for themselves gave me a great deal of personal satisfaction. Hearing them refer to me as their mentor and known as a sort of campus icon was reward enough for my efforts in the classroom.

While I, like most teachers, did not get materially rich through teaching, the experiences I had, the students who became my friends, the good memories of my days as a teacher-professor have afforded me enough pleasure and treasure to last a lifetime. And to think that I, impacted in a positive way the lives of so many young people is something I shall always cherish. I must say from the first day I first set foot in the small one-room schoolhouse in Harlan County to the moment I retired as a professor at Augusta College, I enjoyed teaching. I was happy being with and working with pupils and students. Many referred to me as natural-born teacher who both knew how to teach and loved to teach. Brimming with enthusiasm, I conveyed my love for teaching and books into those pupils/students who came to me for instruction. Perhaps that is why after all those years in the classroom, I enjoy contact with former college students who call, send birthday cards and write me. On trips back to the Augusta area, my wife and I regularly get together to eat and visit with those whom I have taught, including Leigh Ann and Mark Schmitz and their four children, John and Michele Staton and their three boys, Jeff and Lynn Hays and their three children, and Rhonda and Jenny Howard and their mother, Joan. Regularly, I get Christmas and/or birthday cards from Thayer Stamper and his wife, parents of three girls, who is now a minister in Rocky Mount, North Carolina; from Kathie Davenport, now living in Anderson, South Carolina, married and the mother of two children, and from Helen Mulholland, living in Anderson, South Carolina. During the summer of 1996, while traveling throughout Florida and Georgia, my wife and I stopped and had a delightful overnight visit with Jim Glass, an Augusta College student-athlete of mine, who, now married to his college sweetheart and the proud father of Ben and Merydeth, has a Master's degree and is a public school administrator.

Being in the college classroom for twenty-seven years endeared me to a lot of students and them to me—perhaps that is why after all those years teaching college students, I enjoy contacts with young people so much. After moving back to Lexington in the summer of 1994, I became a tutor in the Center of Academic and Tutorial Services (CATS) at the University of Kentucky, tutoring student athletes for several semesters. Since I was born to teach, it came natural to me to tutor UK's student-athletes in one-on-one sessions in 1995 and 1996.

Mr. Paul Taylor and his students at Blanche School, 1948

four women "miners," 1991 (left to right)
Dana Prescott, Elizabeth Bell, Alice Hogan Joy Stanlcup

a group of students inside a coal washer (left rear - Dr. Taylor

class picture of students on trip to mine in Harlan County, 1991
(left rear, Dr. and Mrs. Taylor)

a cavalcade of cars on the wrong road to the mine, 1991